finding ~ heart

PHILOSOPHICAL MEMOIRS, ESSAYS, AND PROSE

by Steven Mayer

Copyright © 2012 by Steven Mayer
All rights reserved.
ISBN: 1466379758
ISBN-13: 9781466379756

For my father
who taught me to seek and find heart

If you don't know the kind of person I am
And I don't know the kind of person you are
A pattern that others made may prevail in the world
And following the wrong god home we may miss our star.

From William Stafford, *A Ritual to Read to Each Other*

Contents

Preface	ix
ROOTS	1
Lazy Summer Days	3
Harvest Time	8
Heading South	11
His Smile	16
Uncommon Sight	20
Never Look Back	24
REMINISCENCES	29
Such a Thought	31
My Littlest Girl	33
The First Day	34
Summer Evening	36
Different Notes	37
Going Home Again	38
The Old Chestnut Tree	42
Forgiveness Finally	44
Out of the Darkness	50
Into the Light	52
Old Soldiers Never Die	54
The Gift	63
Pilgrimage	66

A New Day   70

Dreamer   71

REFLECTIONS   75

Child Within   77

Beauty to Me   78

Old Apple Tree to the North   80

Wildflowers   84

Coming Back   86

A Walk in the Rain   89

Candlelight   90

Listen   91

Homecoming   93

On Power   97

Together   98

Going Right   99

A Few Words   101

RECOGNITIONS   103

You   105

Prayers of a Skeptic   107

Inside Me   110

Finding Heart   112

Believing   114

Final Truth   116

Vital Lies   118

In Praise of Doubt   120

Blessing and Curse	122
An Old Journal Entry	126
Not to Worry	128
High School Reunion	130
In Praise of Hope	136
Bottles in my Cellar	138

REVERENCES — **143**

Wilderness	145
On the Face	147
So Much Wonder and Beauty	148
Tribute	152
Is it Over?	153
Strangers	158
Her Touch	159
At Play	161
Her Way Alone	163
Flowering	165
Wandering Around	166
On Poetry	172
At the Beach	173
Infinite Shore	176

REALIZATIONS — 177

Every Breath is a Miracle	179
Romancing Reincarnation	181
Smiling at the Darkness	185

Best Gifts	186
A Final Thought	187
Acknowledgements	188
About the Author	190
Chronology of Writing	191

Preface

    I love telling stories and taking time to write. I seek to preserve the meaningfulness and magic of existence. My writing often reflects personal history and experiences. It may be light and whimsical, or serious and philosophical. It matters not. What matters is finding *heart*.

    Heart is that inexplicable yet essential human experience when we authentically come into contact with what really matters in life. When we do, it entails inviting others into our private world and entering theirs as invited. Heart is sharing our laughter and tears, unspeakable joys, and senseless pain. It penetrates the core of our being.

    Much is written these days about *soul*. It seems to invoke a sense of hope and invite a metaphysical perspective. It may unnecessarily complicate our being. Moreover, its definitions are many and equivocal. For me, *heart* is a better word. It demystifies my being in the face of life's complications. It speaks to the genuine and real without invoking religious ideation. It surprises. It awakens a deeper, utterly human sense, stripped of philosophical conventions and metaphysical presumptions, in which I transcend the ordinary and discover the extraordinary. I breathe freely and inhale much more than air. I see more clearly, think and feel more deeply, and understand more fully. My imagination is set free to wander in the wonder of all that is—to seek and find *heart*.

    I am a child again, perhaps, or perhaps I am more completely human. Maybe I am just an old man in search of another sunrise. Finding heart sustains me, completes me.

Roots

Lazy Summer Days

When I was a boy, my father, uncle, and grandfather gathered together on rainy, summer Sunday afternoons and played cards for pennies or matchsticks. They sat around a table on our covered front porch, back far enough to avoid the windswept rain, forward enough to allow the easy breeze to lift the blanket of humidity. Our table had room for playing cards, bottles of beer, piles of books, and me. I learned to play poker and gin rummy at an early age. "Full house" and "Jack high straight" were terms of my childhood. My mother disappeared into the kitchen to bake all sorts of goodies, allowing the "boys" to have their time together. These were lazy summer days in my boyhood home in upper New York State.

There was much more: an ideological melting pot of ideas, vigorously advocated and defended. Words were the real playing cards, it seemed, flowing from men with very different points of view. My father was a socialist, unionist, Democrat, pacifist, and a traditional Catholic. My uncle was a political and social conservative, a retired, twenty-three-year Army veteran, a defender of the American dream, and ambivalent toward religion and marriage. My grandfather was a Marxist, an atheist, and an armchair philosopher but foremost a Hungarian; his ethnic pride ran deep. Philosophical contradictions flowed in their blood. They couldn't even agree on what beer to drink or what peanuts or pretzels to buy. Amid the intense crossfire of ideas, I listened and sought understanding—their ideas became my play toys. Most conversations focused on politics, economics, or philosophy but rarely religion, as it tended to elevate blood pressures. Their philosophizing faculty was indeed fecund. The focus that went unnoticed, until its resonance was discovered deep within me years later, was the pure delight of clear articulation and sound argumentation.

Their words haunt me still, some forty years later.

"The capitalist system is flawed: the rich get richer and the poor get poorer. Trapped by economics, the poor are mere pawns of the wealthy, destined to be wage slaves."

"The alternative is worse: government control over income distribution creates more problems than it solves. The poor are free to pursue the American dream."

"It's the American nightmare. You believe that a poor man is lazy and a rich man is ambitious, when history proves you wrong: the rich are greedy and the poor are slaves."

"Without the rich to invest in the economy, there would be no jobs and no middle class."

"The rich are only interested in helping themselves; damn the greater good of society. What is needed is for the poor to revolt and seize control; otherwise, they are doomed to poverty and economic slavery."

"That's nonsense because they cannot fix anything. We need to simply work smarter, not harder, to create economic opportunity."

"We need to overthrow the capitalists but preserve our democracy. We need an economic revolution."

"If we did, we would destroy our democracy. If we want change, use peaceful, political means to achieve it. Use the power of the vote."

Finding Heart   5

They quoted from books and wrote notes in margins and on napkins. Strange, new words demanded explanation. For a young person such as I, these men were indeed interesting company.

They were self-educated with a voracious appetite for knowledge and a deep concern for the common good. They seldom agreed on anything, but they were remarkably patient in listening to each other and keeping their emotions off the playing table. Spirited polemics. Little anger. Pained effort. Little tolerance for poor reasoning or logic. They attacked ideas, not each other. There were always winners at poker but never at ideological poker, which did not require a winner, only players. The game continued indefinitely, save a call to dinner.

The conversations never tired, only shifted topics, philosophy being one of the most compelling.

"Relieving the suffering of the many outweighs the raw, graceless hedonism of a few. There is no moral justification in the unrestricted accumulation of wealth when basic community needs are neglected."

"Even if we agree in principle, what means should we use? Government control and power would breed corruption."

"Morality essentially serves communal utility, not some ethical absolute. Otherwise, how does a society become civilized? We need to be mindful of the dark side of capitalism."

"There are no easy questions or answers."

These were heady thoughts for an eleven-year-old. Thinking back, it is clearer to me today that their thoughts contained conceptual flaws and logical fallacies. No matter. They were thinking hard about important issues, and they became more articulate with each debate.

"War is an invention of society's power holders—it serves no noble end."

"We need to fight to defend our country from tyranny; otherwise, we will lose the freedom we cherish."

"What would the world be like if all nations melted their arms into farm tools to feed the hungry?"

"Such political idealism breeds naiveté. It seduces us into a false security."

Incomplete, incoherent debates, at times, but never boring. On occasion, even religion caught their critical eye.

"Face reality—religion doesn't but escapes into metaphysics. Religion is a crutch for the emotionally weak."

"God smiles at our skepticism and forgives it. He has created us to discover our own purpose in life."

"Look at human suffering and evil—where is God when we need him most?"

"Right here; we just don't recognize him. We expect more of him and less of ourselves in times of hardship, when the opposite thinking is what is really needed."

In their minds, the collision of ideas was healthy and ethically imperative.

Sometimes, the rain stopped suddenly, and I dashed off for a quick bike ride. My thoughts were like the spokes of my wheels, spinning in blurred harmony or maybe chaotic bewilderment. I listened for the distant whistle of the popcorn man or ice cream cart, grabbed a treat, and stopped at the park. Lying on the soft, cool grass, watching the clouds float by and the sun peeking through, I asked my own questions. Hard, uneasy questions. A legacy of philosophical inquiry. It seemed that my father, uncle, and grandfather were smiling over my shoulder.

I am fond of these memories. I remember how the mood shifted when I asked a question or expressed an opinion. They always stopped talking to each other and focused on me, asking me questions to clarify my thoughts. They suggested alternative explanations and asked if I had considered them. Of course, I had not. Implications and consequences? Again, I had seldom considered such. They seemed to be less concerned with my particular ideas and more concerned with my reasoning, logic, and use of words. They never attacked my ideas too vigorously in those early years. That would change as I grew older. Their engagement excited me. It became a rite of adulthood.

My friends visited me and said, "Your family is always arguing." It certainly seemed so. They debated each other, most of the time. Here was an urgency to awaken people to serious dialogue about serious matters and avoid trivial discussions of sports and weather. I lost friends because they became weary of being ideologically engaged. My family's invitation was often unwelcomed and misunderstood, so my friends avoided coming to my home.

The years have created distance and perspective for me. Beyond the conflict of words and the persistent displays of passion were a deep mutual respect for each other and an overriding concern for a better world. As I struggle to recall these exchanges, I realize that these memories are nearly gone now, but their gifts remain with me always.

Harvest Time

The more we remember how we began, the more insightful we become in understanding our life in the present. It may not seem like much, those childhood events, but history is full of surprises. There is wisdom in looking back, because it helps us to learn how to look forward, to preserve the things that matter most.

One of my most vivid memories is harvest time in upper New York State. Every summer as a boy, I spent time at my grandfather's cottage on the shores of Lake Ontario, swimming, wandering the farmlands, sleeping too much, and reading an endless supply of books that continuously appeared next to my bed. My grandfather believed that you should exercise both the mind and body vigorously, and when harvest time arrived, it was time to work hard and long.

When the fruit in the orchards began to ripen, I worked on those farms south of my grandfather's cottage. There were cherries, peaches, pears, and apples to pick. Because I loved to climb, I always had the task of perching myself in the tree tops, bushel basket and rope in hand, balancing to pick with both hands, and lowering the filled baskets to waiting arms below. My grandfather checked on me, knowing that my mother wanted me to stay on the ground, but he knew my heart. I stayed in the tree tops for hours until the trees were bare. My compensation at the end of the week was in baskets of fruit, which my parents transported back to the city.

In the early evenings, neighborhood women gathered in our basement to can the fruit. Large pots boiled on gas burners, sanitizing the canning jars. It was not uncommon to have twenty or more containers of fruit, all peeled and sliced. The aroma of fruit juice was strong. The family recipes for preparing and preserving the fruit, the ingredients added to make the difference in taste, texture, and color, were closely guarded secrets. My job was to clean the pots, floor, and storage cabinets, and to stock the shelves once the jars had cooled. Once stocked, the cabinets reflected vivid colors in clear, glass jars, and the supply was shared throughout the long winter among neighbors. Fresh peaches and cream over hot cereal on a frosty, winter morning invoked memories of harvest time where the bounty of earth and family sustained us. It was a community effort, full of laughter and sweat, life stories, and good humor. I mostly listened but occasionally shared my own dreams of being a farmer someday, of growing and harvesting fruit. No vegetables for me!

Harvesting the fruit was just the beginning, as cornfields awaited. During the hot summer, we played hide and seek in the endless fields, often getting lost, wandering in the wrong direction, and missing dinner. When harvest time came, the fun was over—it was much harder work than picking fruit. The men picked the corn and cut the corn stalks down, and bad corn became hog food. While the men tended to the fields, the women husked corn, sitting in a circle singing songs and sharing stories. My job was to clean up the husking mess, as I was too young to work in the fields. All knew that hard work would be rewarded by a corn fest. The biggest and sweetest cobs were cooked in huge canning pots outside in the farmyard, fresh butter was melted in long troughs, and the corn soaked in them. The patriarchs of the families had the first pick, and then the corn fest started with plenty of music, dance, beer, and laughter. It lasted late into the night, and we lit outdoor lanterns to push back the darkness and fatigue. There was no other food, just corn, and lots of it. In the morning, I awoke with the taste of butter and salt in my mouth, my dirty clothes still on, smelling poorly but with fresh memories of harvest time.

Years later, as these memories begin to fade, the nature of harvest time haunts me. It has much to do with the celebration of life, giving praise to the earth for its bounty, and of communal bonds and shared labor. It taught me to stay close to the earth. It taught me to cherish family. It taught me to work hard and take time to enjoy the fruits of my labors. A harvest of goodness and kindness and love.

Heading South

The year 1951 was a year to forget or perhaps never forget. The winter in New York came early and hard, my father was laid off, and my mother was depressed. My grandfather dreamed of heading south to Florida and invited us to tag along. None of us had ever been there, but it promised much more than bone-chilling cold. He and my mother left in mid-November as the first snow fell. My father and I joined them at Christmas break.

Finding an apartment in West Palm Beach seemed to set the stage for a better future. My mother's postcards spoke of paradise and sunshine. Suddenly, my head was spinning with images of beaches, palm trees, and warm weather. My father hoped to find a carpentry job in Miami. Construction work during the western New York winters had taken its toll on my father's health, and he deserved a change. We might never return to Buffalo. I had never heard of *ambivalence*, but I had a bad case of it: what about my friends, my Cub Scout pack, my spot on the fifth-grade basketball team, and my first true love, Emily, who didn't know that I existed? I coped with the thought of working on a tan instead of shoveling coal and snow. Besides, all the cute girls in Florida wore bikinis, and maybe I could get a real girl friend.

We left uneventfully. We opened the road maps and headed south through Pittsburgh and down through the Blue Ridge Mountains. Horse country. It was green and beautiful; the white fences, like the old country roads, seemed to meander along forever. We stopped for a couple of days at Fort Knox, Kentucky, where my Uncle Steve was stationed in the U.S. Army, guarding all the gold, no doubt. He arranged for us to sleep in one of the barracks and to eat in the mess hall. Seeing a military base for the first time was an incredible experience for a ten-year-old. There were tanks and planes and big guns, and of course, soldiers everywhere. My uncle told me that they were responsible for defending our country, safeguarding democracy, and preserving our freedoms. I stood at attention with him, saluted the flag, pledged allegiance, and pretended that I was a soldier too. Red, white, and blue images danced in my head. I was proud to be an American.

We left early one morning, and by midday, we were in Tennessee. My father had been reading a fat book about the Civil War, full of boring history that he felt compelled to share with me. The road signs inspired him to share historical details related to the area. The "Chattanooga - 20 Miles" sign inspired a lecture: "Grant prevailed against the Confederate forces here," he told me, "allowing Sherman to march south and capture Atlanta." Confederate flags flew at truck stops, schools, and even some churches.

Not much traffic along this lazy, narrow, two-lane country road. About a mile or two past the road sign, we saw an old, gray-haired, black man walking along the highway with a duffel bag and a little boy in hand. They seemed a long way

Finding Heart 13

from nowhere: not many homes or farms out here. As we approached, he turned slightly and waved. My father slowed and asked if they needed a ride. The old man's eyes widened as he looked up and down the highway and then graciously accepted. They sat, quiet and rigid, in the back seat. When I told them that we were from New York, the man appeared to relax. He talked slowly and softly, his Southern accent nearly foreign to our comprehension. After a few minutes, we heard a police siren. My father swore and pulled over. The old man held his head down, pulling the little boy close to him. My father started to get out of the car, but a police officer yelled at him to remain in the car. Another police car arrived, pulled in front of us, and backed up to our front bumper. Three officers approached our car, one on each side, and one immediately in front of us with a shotgun aimed at our windshield.

My father grabbed my hand and told me to be quiet no matter what happened. The police confronted the old man and yelled, "There's a law against hitchhiking in this county; you're in big trouble." My father said, "He wasn't hitchhiking. I offered him a ride." The officer leaned in the door and yelled into my father's face, "You must be a stupid Yankee! Get out of the car!" When he got out of the car, he was pushed down on the hood, handcuffed, and taken to one of the police cars. They told the old man to get out. He was shaking and sweating profusely. The little boy began to cry, and an officer pointed at him, telling him to shut up. The old man was told that he should never ride in "a white car" and that he would be fined and would have to "work it off." He was handed a citation, forcefully turned around, and told to start walking. Lifting the boy into his arms, he walked away and never looked back. One police car left with my father in it. I saw my father struggling to talk to me, but the windows were shut, and the police restrained him. I will never forget the fear I felt as the car faded from sight.

One police car remained with a single officer. I sat alone in our 1948 DeSoto for an eternity, saying a few Hail Marys to hold back the tears. Finally, the officer got out of his car and told me that he was taking me to the police station where my father was in jail. "Jail?" I asked. "That's right, because he gave a ride to a nigger." He told me to get in the police car and "be quiet or else." We drove away, leaving our car on the highway (it was apparently driven to the police station later). Something was very wrong. The Civil War was nearly a hundred years ago. I thought that "we" had won and that President Lincoln's Emancipation Proclamation would result in the end of slavery, and in negroes being treated better.

At the police station, I was told to sit on a bench in the corner of the lobby and not to move. When I asked to see my father, I was told not to talk. Later, they gave me a blanket and said that I would have to sleep on the bench for the night. The police seemed mean spirited and loud and profane. I overheard them laughing about what had happened, and their favorite words were *Yankee* and *nigger*. I was no longer proud to be an American.

I was awakened in the morning by my father hugging me. After he paid a fine equal to all the money in his wallet, he was released and told to get out of the state. There was a large bruise on his face and a cut on the side of his mouth. Later, I realized that he had bruised ribs as well, and that the police had beaten him when he became angry and insisted on knowing where I was. The toughness of his spirit overcame any physical pain. He looked at me and smiled as we walked out of the police station. His smile was etched into my memory forever. We went directly to our car and drove away.

As we crossed the border into Georgia, my father pulled over to the side of the road. I didn't know what to expect, maybe a lecture on not picking up strangers or not disobeying the law. Instead, he told me to never forget what had happened. He knew that I had some idea of prejudice, growing up in a neighborhood with ethnic differences. What I didn't understand was how prejudice could sneak up on you in extreme forms. We talked for quite awhile, but I remember most clearly my father's insistence to judge a man based solely on his actions and character, not on his race or origin. It was a noble ideal that I cherish to this day but was clearly absent from the road signs as we headed south.

His Smile

When I was a boy, my father had an annoying habit. When I thought my weekend was mine to play with friends or to earn extra spending money, he asked if I could work with him to help a neighbor. Some elderly woman needed to have her storm windows put up or taken down, or some sickly person needed his coal shoveled into his cellar for the winter. There were fences to mend, gardens to till, leaves to rake, lawns to mow, snow to shovel, gutters to clean, and houses to paint. Such needs seemed never ending. As soon as some were completed, others appeared to take their place.

I often wondered why people couldn't take care of such tasks themselves. For my father, it was never enough to complete a simple chore. If storm windows had to be removed as winter retreated, why not put up a few window boxes for springtime flower planting? After all, it would brighten the neighborhood. How about a new coat of paint to brighten up things even more? If coal had to be shoveled into a cellar, why not repair the coal bin and clean out the basement? We had the energy, and often the neighbor didn't. For a kid, tolerating a few hours of work was fine, but it generally expanded to fill the entire day. It was painful to watch my friends ride by on their bikes, heading to the park to play baseball or football. Why was I so unblessed?

We never knew most of these neighbors very well. Most of them kept to themselves. My father offered his help (and

My Father
Anthony Mayer
1904 - 1958

mine) with a gracious smile. No thought of compensation. No remote sense of reciprocity, although a freshly baked pie or plate of cookies was never refused. At the end of a long day, we sat together on our front porch, exhausted, enjoying the treats, and talking about the good things we were able to do for people. My father was different, it seemed, from most people—a kind, quietly reverent man with a gentle, warm personality. He worked hard, even after a severe back injury, and seldom complained. When he arose during the night, I heard his painful, barely audible discomfort. My prayers didn't help ease his pain.

Our family knew hardship intimately. Being a carpenter, my father was laid off from major construction jobs during the winter, and he had to survive on infrequent handyman work. It became obvious, as he grew older and his back condition worsened, that employers hired him as a last resort. He found odd jobs, and we stretched our limited resources to survive. I remember winters with no heat or electricity, little food, and limited transportation. He seldom complained about this state of affairs, and he did not permit self-pity or doubt. "God blesses us in ways we don't expect," he said with an easy smile. A strange God, I mused.

A heart attack claimed his life in his early fifties; he sat across from me in our living room, and he simply fell forward to the floor and stopped breathing. Helplessness. The paramedics responded quickly but to no avail. No chance for Catholic last rites. He was gone, forever. Senselessness. I didn't understand my father's God. Though fifty years distant, I can still feel the cold wind on that autumn day, the sky gray and heavy, when we returned his body to the earth. Rage. How could a loving God, his God, take his last breath?

A serious flaw in the divine scheme, indeed. In that moment, the world was dark and strange and empty. Assurances of immortality from the priest became unsettling denials of a stark reality. Impermanence. Loss. No faith. Hope eluded me. Absurdity beckoned. I struggled to capture images of his face, his voice, his smile. With the last shovel of dirt on his grave, I became an atheist. It didn't make sense that God would permit such injustice, and thus it didn't make sense that there was a God.

Years later, I return to the old New York neighborhood. Many things have changed. The towering elm trees are gone, the streets seem narrower, and the houses seem more aged. I walk the sidewalks from which we shoveled snow. Familiar steps. I see the lawns we seeded and mowed, the gardens we tilled and harvested, the window boxes and fences he made, the porches and garages he built and we painted. His white roses still climb to the sun in our old backyard, and his God blesses me in ways I don't expect. The rage is lifted from my soul. The helplessness and emptiness have been replaced with a sustaining sense of peace. I see my father clearly, and behold his smile again.

Uncommon Sight

Grandfathers often hold a special place in our childhood memories. When I was a boy, my grandfather Chorey lived near us on Buffalo's west side. When I completed my daily chores and homework, I visited him in the late afternoon. As I entered the small boarding house room in which he lived, I was drawn into its wonder. The old books, radio, phonograph, chess board, and Persian rug were all treasured fixtures, occupying places of prominence. He was a carpenter by trade and had crafted his wooden desk, dresser, table, headboard, and bookcase.

He often played classical music on his Victrola, teaching me to appreciate various composers and recognize the instruments in the orchestra. Haydn, Mozart, Beethoven, Chopin, and Dvorak were like boyhood friends. There were always open books from which he read to me, explaining the ideas that flowed from Western philosophy. Descartes, Spinoza, Hume, Kant, and Nietzsche were familiar names—their ideas spun wildly in my head. He taught me to play chess: it was a rite of passage, not a mere game. Russian opening and Sicilian defense were common chess strategies for me. Above all, he taught me to cherish my Hungarian heritage. He told me stories of our ancestors and the places they had lived. Some lived in Hungary for over a thousand years, and others were gypsies who migrated there from the high mountains to the east. As he told the stories, he seemed to be in a dream-like state. He often asked if I could see and hear them as he recounted their lives in amazing detail.

We spoke Hungarian in those early days, but that changed when I began struggling in school. My teachers insisted that only English be spoken at home. At first, my grandfather resisted their intrusion, but then he relented and even felt responsible for my impairment. Since he struggled to read English, he insisted that I read to him from his philosophy books. A dictionary was always close by. He loved being my teacher, and I felt this deeply. He enjoyed philosophical discussions and asked questions and expected me to ask mine. He questioned the responses, both mine and his own, which helped me to think carefully about our facts and logic. No idea was safe from critique with me or any one else. Consequently, neighbors avoided my grandfather completely. Philosophers are *lepers*, as I discovered.

MY GRANDFATHER CHOREY AND ME

On Saturday mornings, he was responsible for giving me my allowance, but he was never eager to do so. He expected me to share details about my week with him. Somehow, my grandfather knew things. He knew if I deserved my allowance, what chores I had or hadn't completed, what effort I put into my schoolwork, and what I had learned or not learned from that effort. He knew if I had been kind to people or if I had conflicts and behaved poorly. He knew my hopes and fears intimately, it seemed. I wondered how often my parents whispered such details to him. When I asked, my parents exchanged an odd glance and smile. A silly adult game, I thought.

My grandfather seemed to sense concerns in a strangely different way. As a young boy, I recall climbing up a long extension ladder onto the steep roof of our two-story house while my grandfather and father repaired the roof after a hail storm. I walked to the peak and then along it toward them. My grandfather had his back turned away from me, yet he sensed my presence and calmly talked to me, inviting me to come to him to see the view. He took my hand and put his strong arm around me, showed the wondrous view to me, and slowly took me down the ladder. I quickly learned from my father that it was not a good idea to climb up the ladder.

Western New York is frequently buried in snow in the winter. Shoveling to clear driveways and sidewalks results in huge piles of snow. Once, as a child, I dug a series of tunnels in the snow piles in my backyard. One collapsed and trapped me. Under the heavy snow, it was impossible for me to move. Calling for help brought no response, because my parents were not home. My grandfather sensed that I was in trouble, came to my rescue, dug me out, and poured his homemade peach brandy into me to warm me up. I was told later that he "sensed" my danger and came to find me. When I hurt myself or was upset, he often appeared on the scene.

When I was old enough to work, he knew where I could find a job and encouraged me to pursue it. In fact, he already knew if I would get it. In my teenage years, my parents were estranged from him, so I was forbidden to visit him. There were occasions when I saw him walking alone, and I was drawn to him, almost mystically. I told him that I missed him. He was always kind, shared his concern for me, and knew things about me that I had shared with no one. Before being notified, he knew of my father's death and my pain and offered his comfort. During a visit toward the end of his life, he placed his hand on my pregnant wife's stomach, smiled, and said that she would have a son. A fortuitous prediction? His eyes revealed much more. Uncommon sight.

Never Look Back

"Run fast, far, and never look back."

This thought played through my mind in the days before my high school graduation in Buffalo, New York in 1959. My father had died earlier that year, my mother was deeply depressed, we had nearly exhausted our limited resources, the prospects of employment were bleak, and college was a remote dream. The solution was clear: don't wait for opportunity to find me, go find it. My father had talked about going to California to seek a better life, and his dream became my dream.

Two days after graduation, I set out to hitchhike to California. I stocked the house with groceries and paid two months' rent in advance for my mother, and promised her that I would return for her as soon as I was settled and had a job.

On a cool summer morning, my Uncle Steve drove me to the main east-west highway and slipped a hundred-dollar bill in my pocket. He wished me well, cautioning me to protect myself and use good judgment. With the sun in my face, I stuck out my thumb.

Hitchhiking west was an incredible adventure, filled with interesting people and places. The first ride came from a traveling salesman who was headed for Indiana. He talked as fast as he drove…in excess of 70 miles per hour. We stopped at a diner in Ohio for dinner, and the waitress—a kindly grandmother—gave me a free dessert, perhaps sensing that I was on the road alone. Her kindness surprised me. The salesman later dropped me off in a small town in Indiana, and I found a farmer who let me sleep in his barn that night. Needless to say, I didn't smell too good the next morning when he offered me breakfast. Another surprise. Another kindness.

An elderly couple in an old pickup truck, headed to Iowa, offered me a ride after a few hours. I rode in the back, and they picked up two more kids along the way. As we passed through Chicago, a thunderstorm erupted. They slowed down, and the other kids hopped out. The old couple motioned for me to get in the cab and wrapped a blanket around me with a smile. They wanted to know why I was out on the road. By sharing my story, we connected.

The storm moved on as we crossed the Mississippi River into Iowa. We were headed toward a small town in western Iowa and reached it just before nightfall. After we parted, I walked into a cornfield to find a place to sleep. It was a warm summer night, but it turned cold fast. The stars held me in their incredible embrace. I was alive with dreams dancing in my head and more bug bites the next morning than I cared to remember.

At sunrise, I walked to a truck stop and quickly got a ride with a trucker who was headed west. We drove through Nebraska into Colorado. Seeing the Rocky Mountains for the first time was inspiring. I thought that I could live there and was tempted to stay. The trucker bought me dinner that night and knew by my repeated expressions of gratitude that I deeply appreciated it. He allowed me to sleep in his cab as we continued into Utah. More unexpected kindness.

My only recollection of Utah was its barrenness. The trucker knew all about Mormons, and I knew nothing, so it was an intriguing conversation. I was dropped off in St. George, and I waited most of the day for a ride into Nevada.

A ride finally came from a bunch of college kids headed to Las Vegas. It was good to be included in their energy and dreams for a few hours. Night was approaching, so I opted to get out on the outskirts of Las Vegas where a lot of hitchhikers were camping. Open desert. It was cold, and another kindness was extended when they offered me hot coffee and a sleeping bag. There was a lot of musical talent in this encampment, and we spent the evening around a campfire, singing songs. The sunset was extraordinarily beautiful. Exhausted, I finally retreated to find sleep under an incredible starry sky. I planned to be in California the next day, having spent only twenty dollars and five days on the road.

Early the next morning, I walked through Las Vegas. Though fascinating, it seemed like an alien planet. I checked out a few casinos but moved on quickly. When I left New York, I didn't have a particular destination in California in mind, but it was clear by the interstate highway I was traveling on that I was headed to Los Angeles.

After a few hours, I got a ride from another trucker who drove me all the way into Los Angeles, stopping at a warehouse on the east side of town. He bought me lunch and offered to let me sleep in the warehouse until I found a place to stay.

I reflected on the kindness extended to me along my journey west. It seems that when goodness enters our world, it magnifies the present and sparks a realization of what really matters in life. Those little kindnesses matter. Those friendly smiles. Those heartfelt concerns. The things that strangers didn't have to do but did to help me mattered. I felt incredibly fortunate. I wrote my thoughts on napkins and stuck them in my duffel bag. Years later, I found them in my mother's belongings.

I set out to explore Los Angeles the next morning by foot and bus. The main post office was a few blocks away, and a civil service employment exam was being offered. I took it, passed, and had a job offer within a few days. In the meantime, I found a cheap, one-bedroom apartment. The owner agreed to let me do the yard work for a year in exchange for the rental deposit and the first month's rent. I had a job and a home and still had sixty dollars in my pocket. When I called my mother and told her the news, I learned that worrying about me lifted her out of her depression.

I convinced her to move out west, bought a bus ticket, and returned to Buffalo to get her the next day. We were in Los Angeles in less than a week. The landlord gave her a job cleaning apartments to offset our rent. Another kindness; they just seemed to be flowing our way.

I started my job, bought new clothes, checked out the local beaches, and even enrolled in a class at a community college. I was seventeen, and life was in front of me. Dreams were starting to come true.

Reminiscences

Such a Thought

Another warm summer night surrounds me. I sense a tapestry of crickets, wind, and stars everywhere. A lit candle pushes back the darkness. Gentle music flows through the air. I lie on the carpet near an open window as I write these words. My little girl kneels next to me, and her eyes and hair merge to form an easy beauty, brown and glowing. She places a kiss upon my cheek to say "Good night, Daddy." She squeezes my hand and, with a curious tear, asks if I will ever die. "Not for a very long time," I say. Without hesitation, her little arms tightly encircle my neck, and she whispers softly, "I want you with me forever."

Such a thought for a six-year-old.

Pure and innocent. Possessive and insistent. It will slip away quietly some day, but on this night, it holds her imagination. She dreams of white clouds and pretty angels, singing and playing in a heaven filled with peace and joy, and a loving, kind God. Her face is radiant. She sees us there, too—a family together forever.

My dream of her is different but clear as a beautiful, happy person, content with herself and in love with life. I see the little girl next to me tell me in her eyes and smile that she will be. I can only hope my touch is gentle and her reach is kind.

When I cease to be, when my face and voice fade from memory's grasp, I know that my love will linger on deep within the person she will become. A part of me will be with her forever. I hope it will be my best part, woven into her personality and memories. A part of her will remain with me, those countless, precious gifts in which she touched my life and helped me to be a better father.

Such a thought.

This candlelight vision will not be shared. I smile and hug and kiss her, saying, "Yes, we will be together forever," and her eyes close with a brightness. I sense love everywhere. I lift her into my arms, my little girl, as we dream our dreams of eternity.

My Littlest Girl

Sunshine in every quick smile,
the wind in every moment,
a soft rain in every sadness,
a storm in every stillness:
my littlest girl.

Reflective of nature around her:
a flower in the sun, reaching
with beauty in every season,
sometimes hidden, waiting
to spring into bloom.

Such a delicate variety of color
and life, fragrance and joy, with
an apparent strength as lasting
as eternity, yet tender, gentle,
the bloom may be easily shed.

May my touch be kind.

May no petal drop to the earth.

The First Day

Baths for everyone with shampooed hair screams,
heavy humid air and excited smiles, where curlers
are set and tiny nails trimmed to perfection.

Closets are sprinkled with new clothes and old,
with hints of grass stains and summer bruises, even a
special set lies to greet a fast morning and a bright sun.

Our little children gather around us, with sparkling
eyes and shining faces, hiding uneasy anticipations
of a new school year: listening, learning, and growing.

A family prayer is offered; a sprint to bed is enjoyed,
strong hugs, turned pillows, quick kisses, long stares,
endless questions, pink eyelids, peacefulness.

The first day of school is almost here. The night
passes as quickly as nostalgic summer memories
fade into new dreams of a new year of discovery.

A soft haze of sunlight peeks over the horizon, and
even a rooster would be startled by our children's
early burst to greet this special day, this time of life.

Breakfast is finished, lunches are packed, teeth are brushed, and clothes are carefully fitted with a gentle hand providing the last stroke of beauty.

The moment arrives, that special awakening, consuming our breath with shared hopes and dreams, as small feet hurry out the door, with big anxious eyes.

And so their journey begins, not just to school, but toward the embrace of life with all of its invitations, reaching, stretching, learning, and becoming.

Bless these little children on their way.

Summer Evening

The sound of wind: a brisk and stirring orchestration
of nature's own instruments, fills this quiet summer
evening with a welcomed freshness, sweet to my senses.

My body stretches for yet another breath and lies
motionless, molding to the earth's contour,
as the breeze cools my warm skin.

The peace in this moment is heavy, so easy to embrace
and hug close to my being.

The sounds of the park: quick bursts of excitement
from children playing, laughter from family picnics,
the faint whisperings of young lovers across the lawn.

My body stretches again to see my young children,
sliding, swinging, running together, and my being delights
in a joy ringing from tiny voices, full of life and
innocence.

The music of earth, of nature and life, so full and gentle,
holds me in its grasp, inviting me to celebrate life.

The peace in this moment is heavy, so easy to embrace
and hug close to my being.

Different Notes

Just resting quietly after a long day,
listening to you at the piano, showering
my dry silence with sound. Each note
unique, clear, blending into musical
harmony, so easy and welcomed.

A missed key shatters our peaceful embrace,
yet harmony's flow quickly returns to dance
with our dreams and emotions. Vision gives
way to creative composition, combining
old notes in new ways. Imagination at play.

Can you see? Your piano is a window
into the heart and soul of humanity.
Each person is a unique note, different,
yet essential, blending into community,
human harmony, so needed and welcomed.

You are a note rising with distinctive
sound, and the song of your heart fills
the thin air of existence when your life
becomes entwined with the lives of others,
caring enough to embrace a common purpose.

Going Home Again

Going home again to upper New York State, the land is familiar, though thirty years distant. My roots find nourishment in the lush, green rolling hills, endless farmlands and fruit orchards. I taste the land in each breath of heavy, humid lake air. Even the birds, flowers, trees, and clouds seem unique to this place, haunting me playfully.

Most visitors find themselves taken by the beauty of the Hudson River valley, the Catskills and Adirondacks, the Finger Lakes, and Niagara Falls. For me, the beauty rests in the meandering country roads that lead me back to my birthplace, to places I lived where memories continue to dance around me, inviting me to retrace and discover my past. Along the way, those preciously few grand old homes in Oregon's back country multiply in the New York State landscape. I could live here.

To the far north, the St. Lawrence and her islands are old friends, leading me by the hand to our family reunion at Alexandria Bay. There are new relatives I have not met, along with old stories, photos, letters, and a family history uncovered. They know how to have a real picnic with barbeques, games, swimming, and boating.

Further up the St. Lawrence is Massena where I spent a summer week each year, living with my maternal great aunt, "Grandma" to me. Staying at their summer cottage by the St. Lawrence, I had fields to roam and trees to climb, and a dog of my very own. "Grandma" told me stories of our ancestry, and especially of her younger sister, Rose, my deceased grandmother whom I never knew.

MY GRANDFATHER JOSEPH F. MAYER
HARVESTING TOMATOES ON HIS FARM

Returning to the central part of the state, farmlands roll endlessly over the horizon. My grandfather Mayer's farm is in Rome, a place I stayed and worked for a few weeks each summer. He was the Brew Meister for the Utica Brewery, and on the farm, beer was as plentiful as water.

His farm was a magical place with a huge barn with rope swings and hay for safety nets, orchards and forests for hide and seek, and haystacks in the fields for escape at the end of the day.

Heading west, I close my eyes and smell the fresh air of Lake Canandaigua (among the Finger Lakes), where our family vacationed often in those early days of my childhood. It had a long park by the lake, complete with amusement rides for kids. We rented a lakeside cottage, swam often, picnicked every day, and took boat rides across the lake in the evening. At night, I got to sleep outside under the stars.

At journey's end, I come to my childhood home in Buffalo, an ethnic neighborhood on the lower west side. The old family house shows her weathered age. My father's garden has given way to concrete, the streets have grown narrow, unfenced by the tall elms of my boyhood, even the chestnut tree is gone, and so, too, the birds and squirrels. Only an unfamiliar empty sky remains, staring back at me, sadly. The land seems to have aged much more than I.

Ghosts from my childhood reappear and quickly vanish as I struggle to recapture them. Walks with my grandfather, my small hand held so tightly. My father's gentle manner as he taught me to be joyful in work or play, learning or relaxing. The smell of my mom's apple pies, and her call for supper. Old steps are retraced and my senses are sharpened. Fish on Friday, confessions on Saturday, church bells and mass on Sunday morning, and more catechism and Latin than my head could hold. Gone are the old five-and-ten cent stores, barber shops, drug stores, ice cream parlors, theaters, and baseball fields.

These are warm memories, almost forgotten in the yesterdays of my mind, menaced by a new generation of faces, changes, even to the land itself. Home is not here anymore. It is gone. My visit brings strangeness, distance, coldness, only the Niagara River shows her ancient poise, and gives me the strength to remember. For home is worth remembering, and while the landscape of this place may surely change, the landscape of my heart will not. I will not allow it. Home will always be with me.

The Old Chestnut Tree

Up high, real high, in the old chestnut tree that I climbed as a boy, the world was a magical place. Alone, on a high branch, there was no fear of falling. I was beheld by the wind - fresh and pure, the sky - blue and immense, and the sun - warm and sustaining. The everyday world seemed distant. My senses gave way to imagination.

Dreams mattered more than reality.
Hopes were plentiful and vigorous.
Each unique cloud was a new celebration.
All life was here and now.

Many years have passed. I have grown older and don't climb trees any more. The earth seems colder, less serene, and my senses have deadened. The pace of life is overwhelming. Work consumes me, and obligations burden me. Imagination is a faint memory of childhood.

Dreams lack color and substance.
Hopes are fleeting and elusive.

The present is no cause for celebration.
All life is there and then.

These are heavy, sobering thoughts that bind me to the earth, yet the wind still cools the back of my neck, so I turn to face it and allow myself to be carried away. I climb the old chestnut tree again on this day, up high, real high, to inhale deeply.

Fresh air.
Hopes.
Dreams.
It feels good up here.

Forgiveness Finally

As a teenager, I had a recurring nightmare. I found myself at the top of a deep mine shaft, and a voice far below called my name, seeking rescue. I lowered myself on a rope into the dark abyss, drawn toward the voice, hoping to locate it. At the bottom of the shaft, the voice was omnipresent and strangely familiar. Without warning, the earth shook, and the point of light at the top of the shaft faded. Tons of rock collapsed, crushing me. I awoke in a pool of sweat, flipped my pillow to cool the back of my neck, and hoped to resist the nightmare as I tried to fall back to sleep.

As a young boy, Sunday afternoons often entailed a trip to my Uncle Andy's house for a family picnic, attended by my mother's greater family. There were grilled hot dogs and hamburgers, an array of salads, lots of soda pop for the kids and beer for the adults. We played touch football, badminton, and horseshoes. As evening closed in, the adults felt no pain (from too much drink), and a family fight usually erupted. Ugly words scraped the scabs off old wounds. My mother was generally in the middle of the fight, yelling and berating others. Everyone was accustomed to such drunken outbursts, but my father was embarrassed by them. My Uncle Andy or Uncle Steve would ask my mother to leave and not come back. After pouting for a few weeks but never offering an apology, she was invited back until another fight occurred. Weary of his daughter's tirades, my grandfather finally reprimanded her in front of the entire family, and she stormed off, threatening to never speak to him or the rest of the family again. As a result, we moved from the home owned by my grandfather, a home we had lived in for the first fourteen years of my life. She didn't speak to them again for years, not even at my father's funeral three years later.

My mother's disposition steadily worsened, and it was affected by my father's refusal to engage in her repeated reenactments of her family's sins. When I was sixteen, she began to go to bars nearly every night, drinking, partying, and dating beyond the point of fidelity. Some nights, she did not come home. Her conduct hurt my father deeply, and her temperament was a black hole from which no light was emitted. On one occasion, my father confronted her at a bar, which resulted in a serious beating from her "boyfriend," Larry. When I was called to the bar to help my father, Larry told me to "mind my own business."

My father received little solace from the local parish priest who reminded him that divorce was against church doctrine and that he had to work things out. I complained about my father's beating to our local neighborhood cop, Harold, a gray haired, soon-to-be-retired "nice guy," and was told that there was nothing he could do, though he would not intervene if someone else "did something to right matters." On a dark night, three friends and I confronted Larry and beat him up. My fists were so swollen and bloody that they took weeks to heal. I later heard that we had broken his nose, jaw, and several of his ribs. He was in the hospital for three days. He never accused us of assault because the "word on the street" was that our local godfather told him to leave our family alone. We never saw Larry again.

My father died six months later of a heart attack which I attributed, in part, to heartbreak. My mother then suffered a nervous breakdown and drifted deeper into her black hole of despair and depression. Without other siblings or family to provide support, I was the only person who could help my mother. I somehow managed to do that, though my resentment toward her was apparent. Soon after completing high school, I took her with me to California in search of a new life. She came out of her depression, remarried, and came to enjoy California life. After her second husband's death, I invited her to move from California to Minnesota and later to Oregon. I did the best I could, but my affection toward her was always superficial.

Though it became less frequent, my mine shaft nightmare continued to haunt me. Years later, I participated in a unique therapeutic program that focused on "taking out the garbage smelling up the house"—my inner house. I entered a world of reflection and psychological bloodletting and engaged in peculiar exercises designed to vent repressed emotions. One night, I was carried away in an extraordinary dream. At first, the dream came gently. A soft, pervasive whiteness consumed me, then a maze of vivid colors, swirling slowly, alternately, drawing me into its compelling grasp. In the whiteness, I sensed a profound sense of peace, and in the maze of colors, vitality and power. Dvorak's "New World Symphony" provided the musical score, every note finding its emotional punctuation as the dream unfolded. I came to realize that the whiteness was a canvas and the maze of colors was a palette. I began to apply the colors to the canvas and paint a portrait of the man I wished to be: one with a serious, philosophical furrow upon his brow, integrity in his eyes, a gentle smile in the face of life's complications, the wind of adventure in his hair, the countenance of a wanderer, a gypsy at heart. The sun tanned his face, and the years were kind. I genuinely liked this man except for the sadness in his eyes and the anger in his countenance. No matter how I tried, I could not remove them. The portrait remained incomplete, the colors not quite right, the shapes not exact, the perspective lacking in depth. I struggled to repaint it, sometimes achieving a more-desired effect, other times achieving less. I grew weary and let go of pained effort. I stepped back to appreciate what was on the canvas. In this exquisite, quantum skip of consciousness, insight came: I am both the artist and the artwork. My skill as an artist is a lifelong pursuit, and my artwork will perhaps never be complete nor need to be. It felt good to be so unfinished, but what could I do to undo the sadness in my eyes and the anger in my being?

Near the end of the retreat, we engaged in exercises to release repressed emotions. I alarmed some participants when I beat on a life-sized dummy, blooding my fists and screaming and crying profusely. Buried in my psyche were the images of Larry, my unfaithful mother, and my beaten father. My temperament was a black hole, a bequest from mother to son. In life's conflicts and sports competition, my anger always seemed more extreme than the circumstances justified. After bandaging my fists, I took a walk through the vineyards to reflect. I saw the light at the top of my rational mind beginning to fade, the rocks falling to crush me again, the memory of a wronged childhood. For the first time, I recognized the familiar voice that called me in my nightmare as my mother's. I had to crawl out from under the rocks and climb up the rope to the light. It took so much effort. It was clear to me that the resentment for my mother, a mother whom I helped only because my father expected it of me, who helped me in countless, loving ways as I raised my family, was seriously compromising my desire to be a loving, kind person. Whenever I was around my mother, she sensed this pain and the emotional distance it created between us. It was time to "take out the garbage."

Several years before, my mother had a severe stroke and had to be placed in a nursing home. She could not talk, but she could sing and understand conversations. I tried to visit her daily, but my attention toward her was disingenuous. After my return from the program, I took her in her wheelchair to a nearby rose garden, sat down in front of her, and told her that I wanted to right things between us, things that had separated me from her. I told her that I had acted poorly as a son and that I wanted her to forgive me for being angry toward her. I told her that this anger had distanced me from her, and it interfered with my ability to fully love and appreciate her. We both wept, and I held her in my arms as I told her that I loved her and was grateful for all she did for my family and me. She could not talk, but she tried with gestures, pointing to herself, asking me to forgive her for the pain she caused. I told her I did, completely and forever. Her face softened with a radiant brightness. We held each other for a long time. The sadness in my eyes dissipated, and I have never had the mine shaft nightmare again.

Nine months later, she was gone. She seemed to be clinging to life, hoping that for that day in the rose garden. Her funeral was a simple, graveside service for our family only. My words came easily:

"I hear faded trumpet sounds, drawing me back in time, and once again we see you: of springtime days toiling in our flower garden, of summer days picnicking by the lake, of autumn days harvesting fruit and baking apple pies, and of cold winter days, dressing me warmly. There were long hours of sacrifice, of going without things you needed to help us, of times of pain and joy, and yet you endured, forgave the pain, and found reason for joy.

Thank you, dear mother, for your life, and the life you gave me. I hear another trumpet sound this day, calling you, Mother, calling you home."

Out of the Darkness

We look away. Our eyes never
meet. Only shadows linger. Much
like hand puppets on the wall, our
playful exchange. Fleeting. The
promise of substance fades. Lost,
never found.

We look away. Our voices never
heard. Only echoes linger. Much
like music never played, our words
unspoken. Silent. The present
is empty, the night is long. Lost,
never found.

We look away. Our hands never
touch. Only loneliness lingers. Much
like a pond's reflected images, bending
light away. Oblique. We pass in the
darkness, unimagined. Lost,
never found.

We look away still. Our hearts never
embrace. Only hope lingers. Much
like a moonless night, this curious
human passage. Confused. Our gods
and demons possess us, taunt us. Lost,
never found.

We choose to not look away. Our
eyes and hearts finally meet. Holding
the torch high, we walk out of darkness,
catch the play of light into beauty, life
into promise. Love lingers. Found,
never lost.

Into the Light

Our eyes first meet. We embrace.
The sun rises to warm our face and
heart. Small miracles are dancing
around us. We disbelieve nothing.
We cannot.

Our eyes behold each other. Light
surrounds us. Shadows fade. Gods and
demons flee. Pain vanishes into a caring
heart. We forgive more and regret less.
We must.

Our eyes look beyond. We cherish what
we bring to life. Goodness and hope
abound abundantly. The depth of our
humanity is exposed. Our beauty.
We celebrate.

Our eyes become tearful. We contemplate
the moment. We capture its precious
essence. Compassion flows freely. We
take less, give more. Our being is liberated.
We love.

Into the light, we walk, remain. Out
of the darkness. We discover heart in all
of existence. Our eyes meet. We know all
that needs to be known. All that matters.
We are.

Old Soldiers Never Die

 Sitting alone in his barracks, he knew the end was coming soon. Steve Chorey lied about his age to enter the U.S. Army at seventeen, to escape a bleak childhood, and to avoid the hardships of the Great Depression. Better to see the world and fight for his country. Now, after twenty-three years and attaining the highest rank for an enlisted man, he was retiring. He had been promised that his service would yield a good pension, but his heart knew different: it was time because his time had passed. His youth had been replaced with weathered skin, thinning hair, and an aching body. Echoing his beloved General Douglas MacArthur, he mused that "old soldiers never die, they just fade away." The thought spoke of courage to him, a courage forged under the fire of combat and sacrifice. It gave way to a sense of grace and a peace of mind that he had served well, that his life stood for something.

 The Army was a long way from his impoverished childhood. He only faintly remembered his mother, holding his hand for long walks in Delaware Park in his hometown of Buffalo, New York. She died of pneumonia when Steve was six years old, and because his father, a Hungarian immigrant, was working in the coal mines of Pennsylvania, he and his brothers and sisters were placed in orphanages. As a teen, he lived with his mother's brother in Lackawanna, where he cleaned the family tavern and illegally distilled whiskey in the basement. Steve completed only the third grade of school and was barely literate. The Army provided a chance for him to rise out of his past and hope for a better future. Now, at the end of his military service, his future looked uncertain and uninviting.

Outside the barracks, young recruits marched by, oblivious to the "old soldier." Chanting in cadence, they spoke of resolve and a fighting spirit, of confronting the enemy and prevailing in victory, of toughness and honor and duty. Their words stirred him, though they evoked much different images in the recesses of his mind. He packed his duffel bag carefully, for he would never be back. As he walked outside, the thick, humid air of the Philippines dampened his body. He was accustomed to tropical heat and sweat, having spent most of his military life in the South Pacific. He was also accustomed to the chill and fever that rose out of his tired body, the lingering effects of malaria. Some anopheles mosquito had tasted his blood in the jungles of the Solomon Islands, and that bite would leave its mark for the rest of his life.

A freshly groomed private arrived in a Jeep to pick him up and drive him to the airstrip. A cargo plane was departing for Hawaii, one long hop on his way home to upper New York State. His older sister, Mary, lived there with her husband and son. They had offered him a room in their rented flat and a promise of finding work in the Buffalo area. He had visited there before, taking furloughs to rest and relax from the rigors of war. There was a sobering finality to the lift off, a detachment from a place he would never see again in his lifetime. As the islands below rolled away on the fading western horizon of the expansive blue Pacific, a part of his soul rolled away as well.

Steve Chorey With My Mother (His Sister) And Me

Finding Heart

After moving in with his sister and her family, Steve quickly found a job in a local machine shop. He was a confirmed bachelor and poker player and mostly preferred to be by himself. His nephew quickly learned that the "old soldier" was endowed with serious faults. On hot summer afternoons, he sat in the backyard near the flower beds in an old Adirondack chair with a case of beer and a radio. He listened to Brooklyn Dodger baseball games while lining up empty beer bottles in a single, tight row on the lawn. Mowing lawns and tilling gardens was the work of less-sane people. His sister's scolding rang loud in the heavy, warm air: "Damn it, Steve, all you do is lie around and do nothing. You are nothing but a lazy drunk." Her words did not stir him outwardly, but something deep inside was disrupted.

He faded off to a distant place where the wounds of war were ripped open again. He had fought in the Pacific during World War II, landing in beach assault forces at Guadalcanal, Makin, Kwajalein, Majuro, and Saipan. Holding dying friends, desperately clinging to life, Steve's life was changed forever. He stared into the face of the enemy and saw only a frightened human being clinging to life. Here were momentary bonds of humanity, sensed eye to eye, before common doubts invited brutality, absurdity.

His life was unyielding in its staging of tragedy. In North Korea, he advanced to the rank of Master Sergeant and led combat troops at Heartbreak Ridge, Bloody Ridge, and other infamous sites where the human suffering was tremendous. He seemed to bear the responsibility for the loss of human life alone, and with each loss, friend or enemy, came a loss of soul. In the pain, value and reason were extinguished, evaporated in the smoke of the battlefield. The battlefield moved within. It held his consciousness, creeping in like a thief in the night, to steal his most cherished possessions: his sanity, his deepest hopes, and his easy faith. Uninvited, the dark memories haunted him when the radio and the beer failed to numb him. His peace of mind was delicate, and his sister failed to understand where her incensed words took him.

When his young nephew played war games with friends, Steve disappeared from the backyard. When asked to share war stories, he said that there was nothing to share. One Christmas, his nephew received a set of toy soldiers, complete with jeeps and tanks. Playing war on the green parlor carpet, his nephew invented military strategies to engage the enemy and ensure victory. Great battles ensued. Steve watched in detached silence. On rainy days without a garden in which to escape, he asked him to put the toy soldiers away. His nephew did so without question, sensing that something was wrong. Steve invited him to play gin rummy or poker for pennies or matchsticks. Steve's eyes gradually focused, his smile broke through some cloud cover, and his face relaxed. He fought and found his way back home.

On national holidays, his nephew entered his room to find Steve sitting on the side of the bed, carefully polishing his military medals and pinning them on his uniform, which had been preserved in a sealed bag in the closet. He dressed in a methodical fashion, paying attention to the details of formal military dress. Steve stood proudly on the curb when local parades passed by, wearing his uniform decorated with rows of medals and colorful ribbons, standing at attention and saluting the American flag, holding his nephew's hand tightly. On one occasion, several "old soldiers" in a parade paused, faced him squarely with tears in their eyes and returned his salute. Proud men with a profound reverence for life, not death, with a transparent passion for peace, not war. Steve confided in his nephew that war was glamorized with heroes and victories, with evil enemies and resounding defeats. Steve knew it was creative journalism, and so did his veteran comrades. Their eyes showed that they sought salvation in remembering enough to care and forgetting enough to hope again. These old soldiers had come home, yet they were still finding their way back home. Parts of their souls were left on the battlefield with their fallen comrades.

One summer, his sister, weary of nagging, suggested that Steve find a hobby to rehabilitate his weekends—maybe golf or fishing, something, anything, even a girl friend. Steve relented and bought a fishing rod and a boat. He even bought a small cottage on the shores of Lake Ontario, near the town of Wilson. It was a fair distance from Buffalo, so his sister could visit him only on weekends. When she did, he always went fishing on the lake, alone. His sister was happy, as in her mind, Steve had found a worthwhile pursuit. Using Army binoculars, his nephew could see him sitting in his boat, way out on the lake, with his radio, beer, fishing rod, but no bait! On occasion, Steve invited his nephew to go along, telling his sister that he needed help rowing, even though the boat had an outboard engine. His nephew had to swear to never tell on him, and he never did. Out there on the lake, Steve came to cherish his weekends again. Baseball and beer, the fresh lake air, and gentle lake rhythm embraced him, squeezed out the pain of war, and renewed his hope. Sometimes, he stared off into the distance, entering some distant place in his past. He took off his sunglasses, wiped away the tears, and returned with a smile, asking his nephew for a hug. Radiance was emerging in his face. He learned to find peace without knowing how.

Years later, Steve stood by his seventeen-year-old nephew at the funeral of his nephew's father, a man who opened his home to Steve and worked on Steve's lake cottage. Steve placed his Purple Heart medal in the open casket to show his appreciation. When the words of the Catholic priest became empty, Steve offered the only comfort that felt genuine and meaningful. He knew death intimately. He had found a place within himself where the pain of death transcended into hope. On that gloomy autumn morning, he helped his nephew find that place, too. No talk of God or heaven or an afterlife, just a simple faith that loved ones live on in our memories, their best qualities woven into our personality, and their best thoughts ingrained in our minds. Somehow, somewhere, sometime, their presence is felt and cherished. Their reality becomes our reality.

Two decades later, Steve traveled by train across the country to visit his nephew. He recalled this visit with great fondness. His nephew (and his wife) had taken their family and him to the Oregon coast, and were preoccupied with their two oldest children. Steve took their seven-year-old daughter on long walks down the beach, looking for shells, collecting driftwood, and watching the sandpipers play along the shore. They talked, laughed, told stories, and laughed some more. Sunsets, ocean beaches, fresh air and wind, and the easy laughter of children helped Steve to heal.

One summer, his nephew's family went to visit him at his Lake Ontario cottage. He told family stories, always aided by a beer or two, even some talk of his military service, but never talk of war. He took them to Fort Niagara, recalling the history of the old fort with such amazing detail that they wondered if he had been stationed there in a previous lifetime. When they visited Niagara Falls, Steve sat on a bench and drank in the beauty while his nephew and family hiked around to view the falls. His eyes were no longer distant. The scars of war had healed enough to allow him to enjoy the present and the beauty around him.

The years passed, and at eighty, he married for the first time—it was a short marriage made difficult by age and habits. After separation, Steve escaped to Oregon to visit his nephew again but returned to New York when he learned that his former wife was terminally ill. He stood by her side to provide comfort and hope. He had held people clinging to life on the battlefield, but this was a much different enemy and battlefield. He helped her to stare into the enemy's eyes and endure her last breath in peace.

During most of his later life, he lived alone in Buffalo in a small apartment with sparse furnishings and no phone or TV. All he seemed to need were his old radio, family photos, and beer in his refrigerator. His aged Adirondack chair, its paint nearly worn off, filled his small patio. Lunch drew him daily to the Senior Center on Buffalo's west side to play poker and "win money to pay the rent," as he claimed. In the evenings, he consumed the local newspaper in eager preparation for political debate. Steve sent a postcard each week to his nephew; it was short on words but full of enthusiasm. His life was simple, and he liked it that way. In an effort to share himself more completely, he sent his military medals to his nephew's children as gifts.

It may have been loneliness, the pain of losing friends, failing health, or the dreary, bleak springtime rains of western New York State, but Steve became restless and in need of a more secure environment. Perhaps a change of scenery would lift his aging spirit. He moved to the Soldiers and Airmen's Home in Washington, D.C. and celebrated his last years there. He visited all the memorials with an enduring sense of pride.

He walked past the White House and the Capitol, pausing to reflect on his service to his country, and was often captivated by an American flag waving high in the wind above one of the

STEVE CHOREY AT SOLDIER'S HOME IN WASHINGTON, D.C.

Smithsonian buildings. He stopped and saluted, causing bystanders to stop and admire the "old soldier." His nephew visited him there on many occasions, once taking some of his children and grandchildren to celebrate Steve's ninetieth birthday. He especially enjoyed the children and delighted in their play and energy. He found humor in announcing that he was the "Old Sergeant," that his nephew was a mere "Private" (requiring him to do whatever needed to be done), and that his nephew's wife was "the General" and in charge of the entire operation. He liked it that way.

Steve passed away at the age of ninety-three, and received a full military burial at Arlington Cemetery, attended by his nephew and his nephew's two daughters. A fitting place to honor a proud, good man.

The Gift

Lucerne, Switzerland was a leap back in time. Crossing the long, covered Chapel Bridge into old town, we discovered a maze of cobblestone streets and narrow alleys. Exploring the town, however, had to wait as the Alps loomed in the near distance, drawing us to hike and explore. Beautiful Lake Lucerne at the center of town invited us to take a boat cruise along with a steep, cable train ride up the side of a mountain. Near the end of our stay, it was time to find a few gifts for our family—no chocolate, clothes, or typical tourist trinkets but something uniquely Swiss that spoke to us and would excite our children. We wandered into a little shop filled with a vast assortment of exquisitely crafted wooden music boxes, knowing immediately that our search had ended. At first, we purchased two boxes, but we later returned for one more that was simple and elegant with an enchanting melody. It would occupy a special place in our home.

We took many other trips, but Washington, D.C. was not on our list until my aging Uncle Steve decided to move to the Soldier's Home there. Soon after, we went for a visit. Walking around the Smithsonian Mall, Uncle Steve accompanied us, though he could have been mistaken for one of many homeless persons because of his ragged clothes. He practically lived in his beloved, cream-colored, cable-knit sweater with holes in the sleeves and missing buttons. Over the years, it was always difficult to find gifts for him, but a new sweater was obviously needed. After searching the local stores, we found a handsome replica with a quality label. At the end of our visit, we proudly presented our gift to him, and he accepted it graciously.

A return trip to Washington, D.C. the following year afforded us the opportunity to visit Uncle Steve again, sleep in a Spartan room at the Guest House, eat the cafeteria food, walk around the grounds, and play poker in the evenings. Family photos covered the walls of his small room, and a beautiful quilt made by my wife, displaying pictures of each family member, was spread across his bed. His was a simple life; he was a proud man with a huge heart and the heavy sense that life was winding down. The air chilled in the late afternoon of the second day, and when we went to take our walk, he wore his old cable-knit sweater. When we asked about our gift, he commented that "Harold really liked the new sweater"—he had given it away! He had no need for it, and it was better that one of his friends enjoy it. It was clear that our gift giving was an exercise in futility. He needed nothing except the sun to come up another day to celebrate his quiet presence on the earth.

A few years passed, and he made one final visit to Oregon, traveling the entire distance by train. We loved having him at our home in Eugene. I took him to the "Civil War" football game (University of Oregon versus Oregon State University) in Corvallis, and he drank the bar dry at a friend's tailgate party! He especially loved going to the beach, although walking on the sand was becoming difficult for him. He reminisced about prior visits, especially walking down the beach with our youngest daughter.

We sensed that it might be his last trip to Oregon, given his weakening physical condition, so we wondered once again about a gift. We did not want to buy more stuff that he would discard or give away. He enjoyed looking at our family photo albums and hearing the stories of our trips. His attention to detail was acute, and he often asked me to repeat the most memorable stories. He already had tons of photos in his room, and another album would only add to the clutter.

One evening near the end of his visit, he sat in our front room, relaxing and dozing. I thought that some gentle music would be nice, so I reached for my Swiss music box and placed it near him. He slowly opened his eyes and searched for the sound. I wondered if he had ever seen a music box before, but no matter, he was enchanted. The melody seemed to embrace his soul. I told him the story of finding it in Lucerne. He listened to the music box continuously, it seemed, even opening it first thing the next morning.

We knew that we had finally found a gift for Uncle Steve. At first, he refused it, sensing it was very special to us, but after we insisted, he accepted. The last time we visited him at the Soldier's Home, we noticed he had placed it on a small shelf next to his bed. The soft music carried him away, perhaps, to a different time and space, a place of the heart, inviting reflection and celebration of his life. After he died, I brought the music box back to our home. There are days when I open it and remember the gift of his life to us. He loved completely, and I have little doubt as to why we were inexplicably compelled to purchase a third music box. We bought it for him alone.

Pilgrimage

My grandfather is gone now, but his stories haunt me—ones I heard over fifty years ago, of growing up in a small village in the mountains of eastern Hungary, of swimming in a nearby river, of hiking in the high hills to herd sheep, of a simple life. It was a place of farming and harvest celebrations with gypsy music. His family lived off the land without much else to sustain them. His dreams, however, captivated him, held him each night, dreams of going to America. As a young man, he came to America in the early 1900s, crossing the breadth of Europe on foot and by train, and the Atlantic by ship. He told me of a younger brother who followed him, worked in the coal mines in Pennsylvania, and later returned to Hungary. I recall few details of those stories: no village name, no brother's name, no date of immigration or point of entry.

Age tends to bring increasing curiosity about heritage. I hired a professional genealogist who uncovered my grandfather's 1918 draft record. It gave the name of his brother, Mihaly, who lived in Pittsburgh. Further research produced his immigration record, the change of the family's name from Corej to Chorey, and best of all, the name of their home village of Krivostany, a parish of Stranzke, Slovakia. Cause for excitement. Slovakia had been part of Hungary until 1918. My interest in visiting Hungary piqued. Pieces of the genealogical puzzle were missing, but I had enough information to justify a trip. Given my bond with my grandfather, it felt more like a pilgrimage.

When my wife and I arrived in Budapest, we were on a mission to find my grandfather's birthplace: a remote village 360 kilometers to the northeast, across the border into Slovakia, near the Ukraine, in the foothills of the Carpathian Mountains. We commissioned a young man who spoke English, Hungarian, and Slovakian to take us there. On the morning of

BIRTHPLACE OF GRANDFATHER CHOREY
KRIVOSTANY, SLOVAKIA

our departure, the clouds were dark and foreboding, the rain hard, and the wind chillingly cold. Not the best of days.

Nearly four hours into our trip, we were in the Stranzke region, but there were few signposts to indicate the locations of villages. We thought we were close a few times but to no avail. Seeing hills rising in the distance to the east, we drove toward a small village with a white church on a lush, green hillside. As we approached, we crossed a narrow bridge over a beautiful river, and my heart leapt. The geography matched my grandfather's description. When we stopped to ask, we learned that we had indeed arrived in Krivostany. The village had one main street, about fifteen homes, and a white, Russian Orthodox Church in the middle. As we walked around, the church bells rang exactly at noon. A good omen, I thought.

My first impulse was to find evidence of my family. We searched the area phonebook and the village cemetery, but we found no Corej names. The church was locked, and no priest appeared to live nearby. Hope faded. We walked uphill on the small street to the end, surveying simple homes whose color matched the gray sky above. The flower gardens, however, radiated with color. Walking back, we noticed a cement cross memorial in front of the only vacant house in the village. As we pulled back the vines, we saw an inscription—Mihaly Corej, my grandfather's brother. I wept.

The hard rain stopped, and some women came out to tend their gardens. One indicated that Mihaly's daughter lived a mile down the road, so we hurriedly drove to the place and found an eighty-seven-year-old woman in traditional peasant dress whose facial characteristics closely resembled those of my grandfather. She confirmed that she was Mihaly's daughter. She stated that she had no knowledge of her father having a brother and that her family was Slovakian, not Hungarian.

Our genealogical search may have been flawed. Her eyes and smile haunted me, and her great-granddaughter resembled my oldest daughter. I wondered if my hope obscured my reason and that I was mistaking local ethnic characteristics for family resemblance. Too many wrong answers, it seemed. As we were leaving, the woman said that she had been born in America, returned to Slovakia at the age of two, and that her father had died when she was six, so she had no memory of him or his family. "Born in America? Where?" I asked. "In Pittsburgh," she replied. We had hit the mark, and a distant relative had been found! We drove away, promising to come back someday. The clouds were still dark and foreboding, the rain hard, and the wind chillingly cold, but it had been one of the best of days.

A New Day

My yesterdays were laced
with many dreams, but
my present is crowded
with dreams unwelcomed,
turned away.

I seek to find refuge
in yet another tomorrow,
where dreams will reappear
to inspire vision and excitement
for a new day.

Dreamer

    She is a woman who dreams—often, eagerly, and with pure imagination.

    As a child, she willed her dreams into reality. Seeing colorful flowers in the front of a neighbor's house, she imagined beautifying her home. She picked the flowers and replanted them in her yard. After a severe scolding and apologies, she learned how to plant and nourish flowers properly. To this day, her home overflows with color and fragrance from flower boxes and pots outside and from vases of cut flowers inside. Her presence is everywhere.

    As a young girl, she spent long summer days sharing her imagination with neighbors and friends. Her garage was not a place to store cars and tools but a theater with a stage, props, and curtain. Here, she produced plays and musicals with the neighborhood kids. Performing became a way of acting out her dreams and fantasies. It was a simpler time: a time of lemonade stands, balloon-tire bikes, kites with long tails, skywriting planes, lying on the lawn to smell the grass and flowers, feeling the sun warm your body, and letting the breeze from Puget Sound cool you again.

When early autumn came, she disappeared into the wild blackberry patches, never alone, for her dreams were her companions, leading her by the hand to magical places. There was joy in stained hands and clothes, reflecting her hard work. Even late in life, her berry picking continues with joy, and she shares her harvest in jams and cobblers for all who crave their taste.

I often see this little girl in the woman I married. Carefree. Spontaneous. Fresh and radiant. Her dreams sweep me away, too, calling us to create small miracles and lasting moments in our life together. She didn't hesitate to marry me, even though we had known each other for only eight weeks. In her dreams, she imagined our life together. I don't know if I fell in love with her or her dreams first. She seemed to love fully, not just me but life itself. We had virtually nothing, but no matter—all we needed were a few dreams and some hard work.

She was eager to go wherever our dreams led us. California. Utah. Michigan. Minnesota. Her heart lingered in the Pacific Northwest, her childhood home, so when I was excited about a career move from Minnesota to Boston, I saw the little girl dreaming again. Staring off in the distance, she mused, "Why not just sell our house and move to the Northwest? Every time we visit, you want more time to climb mountains or raft rivers. Besides, it would be good for the kids to be closer to their grandparents." I wanted to go to Boston, so skepticism was my best defense: "It would be tough to make a good career move, and besides, it would be impossible to sell our house on our own in this market." She persisted with imagination. She seemed to know where and how I could seek a job, and within three weeks, I found one in Eugene, Oregon. We put our house up for sale, and with gingerbread in the oven to entice buyers, we sold our house in four days. We packed our three kids in our less-than-reliable Vega and headed west in the winter snows. Pursuing another dream.

Soon after moving to Oregon, I remember her unrestrained excitement as she shared her dream of a country home. Given our limited resources, it was a nightmare to me. She persisted, however, driving into the country every day and no doubt daydreaming. One day, she passed a man who was nailing a For Sale sign on a post for property south of Eugene. When she stopped to ask him about it, he said, "It's for sale, but the sign keeps falling down." Fate? Destiny? Her response was startling. "That's because I'm supposed to buy it!" No talk of price or water or home site access or financing. When she has a dream, there must be a way to make it come true.

With sacrifice, sweat, and a leap of faith, we built our country home. Some friends and family members questioned our sanity and solvency, but no matter, the dreamer never stopped dreaming. It became the place where our children enjoyed their childhood and where we now enjoy sunsets together. Wild blackberries, daisies, and wildflowers fill the lower meadows, and ferns, tall firs, and solitude flourish above us. The birds seem to sing in the morning just for her. The deer and raccoons find refuge here in the evenings, and the night sky is full of stars and magic. What better place for dreaming?

People who dream have goodness in their being, a faith in a better tomorrow, and a trust in possibility—so does this woman. I have seen her provide countless hours of service to benefit others, counsel troubled friends, care for dying ones, help strangers in need, teach our children, and share herself fully in whatever cause inspires her. In all of her care giving, her dreams provide a profound sense of purpose and meaning. Those closest to her can clearly see that her greatest gift to others is her eager invitation to dream. Without dreams, she would say, life is shallow and mundane. She is right, though it took me years to grasp such a simple, elusive truth. We become our dreams.

Now, as the sun begins to set in our lives, she reaches for new dreams still, to cope with change. It is as natural for her as breathing and stretching her body in the early morning. Often, her dreams seem beyond reach, and I see the little girl in her smile again. She is still willing to dance on the childhood stage, to pick her blackberries, and to weave her magic. She has an unwavering faith that reality can be shaped, even created. I lie here this morning watching her sleep peacefully and wondering what dreams she will share with me today.

Reflections

Child Within

Freedom, wonder, and imagination flourished in our springtime, with days lived eagerly, and tomorrows captured in dreams. Our spirit yawned and inhaled fresh resilience, moving openly, nakedly in Eden's garden, unveiling its spontaneity with emotions very close to the earth.

Our vision is tinted now, our movement confined. Somewhere culture's heavy net caught me and you. Now the sun passes swiftly. Tomorrow quickens into today, and today, like most days, is lived less. Pacing, we deny our captivity.

There is a child within, seeking escape if only for a moment. A young voice reaching back into our yesterdays for a new day's message: take time to wonder, seize freedom to spring, and hope to dream again.

Let the child be reborn. Let him crawl into our senses, for only then do we sense a yearning to embrace life and feel its pulse again. We become whole, one with all that is, and want our future.

Beauty to Me

What is beauty to me? My heart stirs. Mere verse cannot capture its elusive touch, for only when I pause to accept nature's gifts are my senses filled with glimpses of the beautiful in and around me, beholding and beheld.

From flower to flower in earnest haste, this tiny bee, relentless in her singleness of purpose, laboring in the goodness of her creation… Is this not beauty?

And long shadows of the robin cast in the early sunrise of a new day, eager to unfold her being, giving in the goodness of her creation… Is this not beauty?

Within the tall grass rests the quiet presence of the doe, graceful, vulnerable, daring, reaching in the goodness of her creation… Is this not beauty?

And here, there, a spring, a flutter in a breath of wind is the butterfly's erratic flight, full of color, in the goodness of her creation… Is this not beauty?

Do you see? This tiny bee, eager robin, graceful doe, and butterfly are reflections of beauty. In all these wonders, I discover you...

the singleness of purpose, untiring...
the sacrifice of life for life, caring...
the graceful solemnity of faith, reaching...
and a bursting flight of life, lived fully.

As I lie here this day, I am filled with a deep sense of love and celebration. You see my dear, nature speaks to me of you, and the warmth of the sun touches me as you touch my soul, for you are beauty to me.

Old Apple Tree to the North

The stars in the clear night sky held me as I rested after a long day of work. We had sold our home, our family of five was living in a small apartment, and I spent every evening and weekend working on our future home, shovel or hammer in hand. The daily routine was simple: awake in the morning, drive to the apartment to shower and eat breakfast with my family, go to my full-time job, come home and eat dinner with my family, and go to our future home site for the rest of the evening or weekend, camping there to conserve time.

Early one spring morning, as I was waking up, I saw them, so graceful in flight: a pair of robins. They came with a sense of purpose, circling the branches of the old apple tree to the north of our future home site. It was here they would make their small nest with such delicate care to shelter the life they together would give the earth, as surely as the apple blossoms around them would give the fruit.

When we moved to western Oregon, we dreamed of building a home in the country. In our second year, we found and purchased nearly ten acres of property with a beautiful view, a short distance from Eugene. Limited resources did not deter us; it invited creativity along with debt. We were determined to clear a building site by the following year, as soon as the springtime rains lessened, but as the seasons changed, our dream became a nightmare. The property became a dense, nearly impassable landscape, filled with winter springs and mud holes, wild cow parsnips growing everywhere to eight feet, intertwined with blackberry vines, poison oak, thistle weeds, tall grass, and mazes of scrub oak on the edge of a Douglas Fir forest. Clearing the land was exhausting. Developing a spring-fed water system, a septic tank, drain field, and a road into the site took nearly four months of work before the home site could be developed and home construction could begin.

Exhaustion can foster doubts about your sanity. Dreams, however, can surprisingly preserve sanity, even when your body is worn out and covered with poison oak. Hard work and long hours were the way dreams came true.

I took breaks in the shade of the old apple tree. The robins never rested. They had constructed a strong nest in tight, high branches, with considerable effort. The sun grew warmer, and then, miracle upon miracle, first one, then another, and finally a third little head appeared, begging for food in each breath of life. They woke me each morning at dawn. The robins' shared labor to provide for their newborns was endless. Small miracles of nature were unfolding before me.

By late August (almost too late to start home construction because Oregon's rainy season would be upon us in two months), we poured cement for the foundation. No remote thought of delaying construction until the following year. No rest either. We took lumber from trees we had cut down and built the subfloor before Labor Day. With the radio blasting, we danced on the open floor to celebrate. A seventy-year-old carpenter friend agreed to build our home with my help. The entire family helped to haul lumber, nail down floors, walls, rafters, and bracing. We were in a race to enclose the house before the winter rains arrived in early November. I put on a cedar shake roof while our carpenter and his son put up redwood siding, Linda and the kids primed and painted the windows, and except for a brief shower, the house was enclosed by Thanksgiving. Exhausted but jubilant, we celebrated again. Our house looked like a home.

In the embrace of the old apple tree that gave its fruit to us, the robins watched as their young ones grew and spread their untested wings, taking flight in ever-widening explorations. There were perils beyond the branches, but nature must have her way. We saw first one, then another, and finally the last offspring rise on a wind from the west and vanish over the horizon without a glance toward the apple tree.

The "to do" lists were lengthy, and at times, annoying, as was the scheduling of contractors hired to do what we couldn't. Our carpenter friend built the kitchen and bathroom cabinets, and I laid the oak hardwood floor. We finally completed most of the inside projects and moved in just before Christmas. Another celebration. There was still molding, painting, wallpapering, and carpeting to do, but our home in the country was built.

We raised our children there. It was a delight and at times a struggle to watch them grow and develop their independence. We watched them leave for college and return, and later leave and not return. Our home seemed empty without them. Later, our children had families of their own. They returned, but it was no longer "their home." Even so, the homecomings were cause for celebration and for building a tree house and playhouse for our grandchildren.

I remember the robins staying close to the nest, watching their young ones fly from sight and not return. It seemed that they were watching those spring days haunt them again, for it is their gift to remember and cherish the life they gave, the miracle they are. With autumn's setting sun, they flew away together to the southwest beyond the distant ridge but not without a final glance toward the old apple tree.

It is hard to imagine that we will ever sell our home. Too many cherished memories linger here. We plan to live our last days here. When we travel to distant places, we always glance back at our home, enjoying the beauty of the natural setting with an enduring sense of place.

Wildflowers

As a young girl, you loved to search for wildflowers, sometimes hidden in the meadow, barely stretching through the tall grass to touch the sun. The most beautiful were always the most difficult to discover, struggling among the weeds and blackberry vines, though their stems were strong and steady, and their color vivid and pure. I have fond memories of seeing you, sitting alone in the meadow on those summer afternoons, talking to the animals, and enjoying the beauty of the wildflowers in their natural setting.

As a young woman, you are a wildflower, sometimes hidden in the landscape of life, stretching barely through self-doubt, fears to touch the sun. You will endure the struggles, heartaches in your unfolding, blossoming, to become one of the most beautiful, fragrant, colorful, vital, and life giving. This is neither a mere hope nor a fading metaphor but a simple vision, vivid and pure. There will be an after-mist in the sun-filled meadows of your life and a rainbow to crown the radiance you will discover in yourself.

We love you deeply, though distance separates us. We wish we could hug you and bear struggles for you, but we cannot. You, alone, must stretch to touch the sun to become whomever you choose to become, even a wildflower in the rainbow's glow.

Coming Back

My son left Oregon on a Saturday afternoon to drive to Santa Barbara to visit his girlfriend. He needed to be back at college in Utah on Monday morning. Over fifteen hundred miles of driving, mostly at night with little sleep and less sense. The hard rock music that had annoyed me during his teenage years was now a strange solace, giving me hope that it would keep him awake. As he left, he could barely endure the typical parental cautions we gave about using good judgment and not driving when exhausted. His reply offered little comfort: "I have things under control, Dad, don't worry." I went to bed early that night, anxious about the welfare of my son, and found it nearly impossible to sleep.

During his teenage years, we had grown apart. His adolescence was a time of tension between us, a time of forming his own identity. During the same period, I struggled with my own midlife crises, wondering if my life choices were fulfilling. His adolescence and my midlife collided. For my son and me, it seemed like an experiment gone terribly bad.

I reflected on early times, of a young, gentle boy who was eager to learn, who excelled in science, math and piano, and who enjoyed sports. A voice reminded me that the same boy was there in the teenager he had become. Our list of high expectations for him plagued me. Parents tend to respond to unmet expectations in one of two ways: tear up the list or tear up the kid. Most often, I was guilty of the latter, which inevitably led to angry exchanges. I was haunted by the fear of permanently alienating him, overreacting to normal developmental issues, and failing to perceive the strength of his character, much less appreciate it.

My wife was already asleep, but I was restless, drifting in and out of sleep. A dream swept me away, a dream so real that I seemed to be conscious. In the dream, a phone call came in the middle of the night. There had been an accident and my son had been seriously injured. I found myself springing outside of my body, gliding in the still, cold night air above the highway, looking down at the wreckage, and a battered body, clinging to life—my son —his eyes filled with pain, desperation, and fear. A stranger knelt beside him, helplessly, to offer comfort. The chilling draft of eternity pierced my being, and I saw my son's eyes close with a final breath. He was gone.

I felt a hand on my shoulder and turned to see a person in a pure, white light, his arm around my son. A gentle peace filled my being. He asked if I wanted my son back but paused to add that his return might bring sadness and heartache. His question was simple: "Can you love and accept him?" My son looked directly at me, his eyes asking the same question. I knew he wanted to come back.

My reply was quick and firm: "Yes, I can love and accept him. We want him back; we want our son." My son knew my heart in that moment, and I knew his. In some recess of my being, I wondered if my resolve would endure; I hoped it would. In that exquisite moment, my son was released into my arms, and in embracing him, I came to understand what truly matters in this life. The dream slipped away. I took a deep breath and squeezed my wife's hand, wiping the tears from my eyes.

This dream changed my life. I came to celebrate the differences between my son and me. Years later, the wisdom of the dream continues to flow to me, inarticulate yet indelible in its touch. My son has become a better man than I. His accomplishments are less important now, and I cherish him and enjoy the person he has chosen to become.

A Walk in the Rain

An early evening walk
with my wife
in the rain through
a Portland neighborhood:

we enjoy easy conversation
and uneasy faith.

Our laughter and heartache
are colorful celebrations of
living simply yet another day
in delightful obscurity.

Each step takes us beyond
the distancing judgment
of others, supposed friends.

Our hands clasp, eyes meet
with an intimacy of understanding,
deeply known but unshared. Our
walking slows, embracing:

we enjoy uneasy conversation
and easy faith.

Candlelight

Born, barely lit, barely bright
in the darkness, the flame flickers
and fades. The wind is indifferent,
suddenly unfair. A trail of smoke
rises, delicately disappears.

My rage brings flame fleetingly
to the candle again, lifts it high
against the darkness, reclaims it
from extinction's grasp. Reborn,
not forever, in memory alone.

No greater pain consumes us
than the death of a child, precious,
innocent, helpless. Neither purpose
nor faith is imagined. Senseless.
Raising my fist, I rage at the universe.

And as my rage burns deep, a
different candle is lit, holding back
the darkness. Faintly lighting my
presence is *hope*, gentle and pure,
giving me the courage to go on.

Listen

Listen, my friend…

>the haunting whispers of seashores,
>the chilling echoes of forests,
>the gentle music of meadows,
>the serene thunder of mountains,
>the relentless cries of cities,
>
>>at once captivating, vanishing…
>>this voice of the earth.

Listen still, my brother…

>the whispers speak of new life,
>the echoes reveal aloneness, independence,
>the music gives rise to beauty,
>the thunder announces the birth of vision,
>the cities release our common pain and joy,
>
>>at once captivating, vanishing…
>>this voice of humanity.

Further yet, my companion, listen…

new life reveals new days,
independence brings unique days,
beauty invites meaning to all days,
vision promises better days,
pain and joy accompany every day,

at once captivating, vanishing…
this voice of mine.

Listen.

Homecoming

(This prose is not a literal description of a physical place. It is a metaphorical description of my inner self.)

Often when life's complications, pressures, and pace bear down upon us, we can turn inward, homeward. For me, the journey is solitary, and the old familiar road, though traveled many times before, is never tiresome. Here are open arms to welcome me, to hug me again, and to bring a deepening sense of acceptance, comfort, and peace.

When I am nearly home, I pause to view it fully from a distance, realizing that it has become a spacious place with many rooms, each unique and different in size and furnishings, purpose, and promise. All are comfortable and inviting. Each has large, uncurtained windows to draw in light and colorful flower boxes to draw in nature's color. I may enter the front or back door; it matters not, for both are unlocked. Bright, wide hallways are behind them, with walls displaying treasured art and family pictures. Love and beauty are within these walls. There are also small signs scattered about that give reason to pause and ponder: "Home is a communion of the spirit" (Peter Megargee Brown), "For without the private world of retreat, man becomes virtually an unbalanced creature" (Eleanor McMillen Brown), "Much of the character of every man may be read in his house" (John Ruskin), "There is no reason, either in prose or in rhyme, why a whole house should not be a poem" (Ella Church Rodman). I need to take time to reflect upon these signs more often.

I spend most of my time in the large, open living room. It has a large bay window to shower in the color of the countryside. It is uncluttered. There is a hardwood floor with plenty of room to dance or exercise, so much so that you cannot resist the urge to be playful, joyful, even adolescent. There are comfortable sofas and chairs, covered with garden-fresh fabrics that invite relaxation, conversation, and laughter. My family and friends know this room well.

My library is a quiet, nearly sacred place in my home, with high ceilings and shelves, filled with volumes of knowledge and imagination where I like to browse. It has thick carpeting, comfortable chairs, and leaded-glass windows with shutters to cast light in shades and colors. Much of the time I spend here is alone. Intellectual integrity and curiosity flourish here. I write these words here. My family is respectful of my wish to spend time here and seldom enter because of the fear of uneasy conversations. I do not insist that they enter my library.

Other rooms in my home are visited less frequently. Upstairs, my bedroom is a place to rest, relax, and recover at day's end, at journey's end. It is a sensual place whose privacy will not be breached. There is a warm fire in the hearth, fresh bedding, colorful quilts, soft music, candlelight, and love to push back the darkness.

My attic is filled with joyous litter: old photos, letters, journals, mementos, and artifacts collected along life's journey. Here is a place to cherish my past and realize that the presence entails more than sitting in my living room. My family loves it here.

Down the stairs to my basement, I discover not a dark and dreary place but one that is clean and open. Its thick walls are the foundation of my home. I sense strength, meaning, and timelessness here. I sense the presence of my parents, uncle, and grandfather. I sense my beginnings here.

Wandering around my home, I often enter rooms reserved for each of my children and my times with them. The walls are filled with photos of their growth and unfolding. The closets still hold some of their favorite clothes and childhood memorabilia.

My front porch is wide and long, covered to shield me from the rain, with hanging flower baskets. I often sit in my rocker here to enjoy my memories of mountains and rivers, of the joys of working and teaching, of giving and caring for others in their journeys, especially their homecomings, and of the beautiful woman who has shared her life with me.

Sometimes, I discover a new room, one that has always existed yet remains unexplored. It may be dark, though I enter unafraid, for it is still within the walls of my secure home. Those closest to me may point me in its direction. I come to realize that my home is often more than it appears to be.

I confess to having a secret place in the center of my home: a sunroom with open windows for walls, drawing in fresh air, sunlight, and the stars at night. Such peculiar architecture. Here I am totally immersed in stillness and warmth, giving way to reflection and wholeness of self, inviting the mystical and wondrous. There is no activity here, only being. No others, only me. I am vulnerable and unprotected, yet nurtured in this space. I never talk or even think here, only listen and feel. I am one with all that is, ultimately and intimately. "Dream delivers us to dream, and there is no end to illusion" (Ralph Waldo Emerson).

Friends and family are always welcome in my home, though most view it only as a living room. I offer invitations to the library, attic, or basement, but few accept. Spending too much time in the living room, my friends become strangers, and I, a stranger to them. I seek to explore the rooms of my friends' homes, but they seem confined mostly to their living rooms as well.

Homecomings are cherished, for they bring a depth of perspective, a sense of purpose to life itself, and a sense of identity to my being. Goodness abounds here, and my heart is untroubled. Where else would I live? In my library, I ponder whether this wondrous place will endure, and I am laced with doubts. Such doubts dissipate in the pure light of my sunroom, and I embrace hope again.

I enjoy the home that I have built. In my yard and gardens, there is ample space for all of the earth's creations, for the flowers and weeds, for the lawn and exposed earth. I welcome the sunshine and the rain, the stars and the moon, the mystery and wonder.

This is my home. This is where I live.

On Power

The exercise of power can be a frightening revelation
of our inner self. Its abuse can become infectious:
a cancer of the spirit, compressing all worth to exalt
one's intuition and status, delighting in intimidation,
inviting confrontation, feasting on violence, boasting
of genius. Above all, beneath none, self deity is
inevitable with its consuming appetite for grandiosity.

Abuse of power is universally transparent: unleashed
aggression leads to barbarity, ensnarling our psyche,
preying on all weakness, passionately righteous.
Lasting cure is improbable, for peace is merely
a seductive prelude to recoil and attack. Can the
gentle person survive? He who abuses power must
win, while he who falls prey must endure and survive.

The gentle person resists the gambit of abusive power,
concealing personal power in forbearance, kindness,
freely witnessed, unconditional, void of contempt and
hatred. The gentle person finds strength in the virtue of
sacrifice, not of the things that matter most, but of the
things that matter least.

He who abuses power may prevail in the moment,
but his triumph is fleeting. He who is gentle and endures
past the moment, will know triumph in the quiet hours
of life. He shall be a victor.

Together

Reason should never seek
to extinguish passion.
Reason should seek to refine
the brilliance of passion.

Passion should never seek
to overwhelm reason.
Passion should seek to
magnify the clarity of reason.

Reason without passion
is cold, damp, and impotent.
Passion without reason
is a hot, but dying ember.

Together, they bring
meaning to what is human.

Going Right

It's a dark, rainy day. The earth is drinking deeply. It's a good day to stay inside and read a good book or listen to good music. I pick up my guitar and begin to play a few chords, poorly. My teacher's voice reminds me of the need for patience and repetition. No mention of frustration and arthritis. The challenge seems overwhelming.

The primary problem, my teacher muses, is that I need to move to the right side of my brain and stop thinking about playing, flow with the music, and "become one" with my guitar. Let the music lead me to the chords, and stop looking at my fingers to find the chords. When I do, I am stuck in and inhibited by my left brain. I wonder if there is any scientific credibility to the left brain - right brain dichotomy or if it is merely a popular piece of metaphysical dribble.

Assuming some truth to the notion, it seems that I have spent nearly all of my life on the left side of my brain. Supposedly, the left side is involved in analytical work, the business of science on the top end, and the routine rigors of living on the bottom end. I had thought that my personal writings had lead me into right-brain territory, but upon reflection, it is mostly philosophical (left brain) and invokes my imagination only fleetingly when considering style and format. I thought that listening to good music or reading poetry might be a venture into the right brain, but when "I think about it," I am most often "thinking about" the music or poetry. It seems that I have been caged in the left side.

I find myself pacing the cage. I want to learn to play the guitar well, but I am inhibited by my lack of dexterity and improvisation. I rest my guitar upon my lap, begin to play a few chords and don't think about it but give in to the "pulse" of the experience. Damn. I find myself thinking about not thinking! This is not an easy transition. I wonder if my age is a factor, but again, I'm thinking too much. How do you escape or even suspend the left side? I don't have a clue. Maybe being clueless is a good thing.

I imagine that learning to drive again is a helpful metaphor. Going left is a wide gradual sweep with the line marker next to me—an easy, open turn, it seems. Going right is a quicker, tighter move without a clear view of the line marker, and I find myself "bumping the curb" repeatedly when trying to play the guitar. My brain feels numb when I don't think about my guitar playing. No steering wheel or accelerator or brakes. No map or compass. No bridge across to the right side.

The only thing I know is that I seem to be "going right" without understanding how best to do it or what is going on. It is a clumsy leap of blind faith, up a steep hill. I practice "feeling" the music and flowing intuitively to the chords. I laugh at being inept and awkward. I discover that my imagination is becoming more vivid, my emotions more intense, my breathing slower, and my being more relaxed. A hard space to sustain, but an amazing one.

I wish I had taken this trip a long time ago, going right.

A Few Words for My Grandchildren

A person with a good heart is infinitely more inspiring than one with a strong mind. Though the differences may be subtle, we may find those with strong minds and cold hearts, and those with soft heads and warm hearts. While I delight in what each offers, I opt for the latter. There appears to be greater virtue in actions flowing from good hearts compared to the understanding flowing from strong minds. A person with a good heart and a strong mind is a pure delight for all humanity. A person with a cold heart is a tragedy for their loss becomes our loss. Seek out good-hearted people as friends, teachers, and work associates, and your life will be richer.

Recognitions

You

You, so wondrously, playfully
mysterious, are the final paradox.
Universes beyond and within,
explored unto infinity, are shores
of shifting sand between which
the sea of time ebbs and flows,
on which, floating, adrift for a
precious moment is your being.

This curious human awakening,
inexplicably transparent, paradoxical:
simple and complex, free and bound,
alone and relational, good and evil,
strong and weak, selfish and caring,
color and darkness, growth and entropy,
and infinitely more.

In the erratic pulse of being,
each difference is unique,
each expression is original,
each creation is mystical,
each movement is meaningful,
each consequence is endless.

You are of profound, enduring value,
worth, enhanced by intimacy with all
that is and will be, forsaking guilt toward
the past for what might have been, anxiety
toward the future for what might become,
celebrating the reality of the present and
the paradox of you.

Prayers of a Skeptic

(This prose was written nearly three decades ago at a time when I was struggling to develop religious faith and participate in a religious community.)

O God: How I wish you exist and could sense the inner longings of my heart in my reach to thee. Even as hope softens the heavy air of stillness, it continues to whisper: Are you here, there, anywhere, somewhere?

And if you hear my words, see my darkness, know my heart, and understand the gnawing doubt enveloping my quest, then: Why, oh, why don't you speak? Can I not hear? Or am I more alone than I care to acknowledge?

I reach to thee respectfully, silencing my skeptic's voice and willingly suspending my disbelief, acknowledging the possibility of your existence, hoping my faithful prayer is not in vain.

At once, there is a breath of freedom and a vision of nothingness. I am beginning to distrust even the slightest substance from within, hinting of your presence. How can I know? Will I ever enjoy the delight of revelation? Will the skeptic ever find rest?

In my search, I cannot know that thou are not, even if this vast nagging silence prompts negation, my inner self permits no such presumption, but likewise, my doubt prohibits a leap to thee.

For thou, not me, art the cause of my eclipse. It is you alone who chooses to be silent, and if there is wisdom in silence, it is not mine to know, for now this silence pervades me, too, and I am as thee.

O God: You tempt me so, beckoning me to seek you, but eluding my touch, causing me to wonder about existence and meaning, inviting me to give in to negation and aloneness, silencing my hopeful voice in the face of suffering and injustice.

You tempt me so, playing with me as you seem to do, for I seldom find, much less understand even the remotest purpose for your absence from my life, for I have rage at the absurdity of it all, raising an irreverent fist toward you, for I question not where, but what you are?

You tempt me so.

O God: Where art thou? Further yet, art thou?

I have sought thee in the writings of philosophers and prophets, between the lines of scientific explanation, in the wonder and beauty of nature, in the intimate confessions of believers. I have not found thee.

When I have not sought thee, I have felt a tremor in my being, turning me away from external proofs, turning me inward toward a deep, warm, pure light, shining undeniably beyond delusion and darkness.

I have wondered: Have I found thee? Is the divine manifest only within and not outside my being? I do not know. I know only that I am more than I appear to be. I know what I sense deep within and imagine thy smile in the midst of my search, asking: Where art thou? Art thou?

Inside Me

There is a philosopher inside me, alone, sometimes lost but never fearful:

> wandering in a vast landscape of ideas and perspectives, critically considered, and prudently accepted or rejected,

> residing in profound silence percolating with creative contemplations.

Here is a realist who often pauses to challenge a naïve sense of reality, searching for a crack in the cosmic egg:

> consumed by the ethical and pragmatic, but not to the exclusion of philosophical abstraction,

> taken by existentialism's sensibility and its appeal to free will and self determination,

> suspicious of logical empiricism's endless reductions, yet honoring and affirming the value of science,

relentlessly analytical, delighting in a steady stream of searching questions, forever tentative yet tenacious in pursuit of truth and meaning,

fleetingly involved in a tempestuous romance with mysticism, occasionally yielding to her seductive siren,

and cautiously discovering the spiritual and religious around me, within me, balancing faith and reason, yet ceaselessly resisting their inviting dogma.

I trust the darkness within me, around me, for out of it comes light—penetrating and illuminating—with fleeting glimpses of the sacred and holy, and with a resonance of passion to fully enjoy the gift of my existence.

I trust that there is a philosopher in each of us. A voice of reason to which we can listen without fear. A voice that also encourages us to discover *heart*.

Finding Heart

Faith springs from a hope that the universe is more wondrous than imagined by science and that human existence is connected to it in some eternal, infinite manner. This ancient hope rising with the dawn of humanity is nurtured further by fleeting sensations in human experience, seemingly revealing this wonder to us. We believe, not knowing exactly what to believe but believing nevertheless in something greater than ourselves, something greater than our ordinary senses can detect, something sufficient to suspend disbelief in favor of belief.

Educated within the paradigm of science, my thinking demanded both rationality and prudence. To entertain a leap of religious faith, I had to rationalize it. I struggled to find a place in a particular religion for me. My mind was both my guardian and my refuge, ensuring critical thinking in considering metaphysical and ethical propositions. While relying primarily on analytic philosophy, I brought the universe (or rather my naïve perception of reality) "into me" and attempted to make precise sense out of any assertions requiring faith. I sought knowledge and certainty and found that neither was possible. Any prospect of faith appeared to be troubled and neurotic.

The prospect of delusion seemed more likely. Finally, I realized that my search was egocentric and relied exclusively on the strength of my intellect. I wondered if I might be the cause of my own eclipse.

Later in life, exhausted by my quest for rationalized faith, I shifted my perspective. My search became less centered in intellect and more centered in wonder, less focused on the known and more on the unknown. It was no longer egocentric but *being-peripheric*, reaching into the mystery and intrigue of all that is. I no longer endeavored to find a place in a particular religion, an increasingly confining place that subverts my leap of faith. Now, I seek a place for the religious in me, a place for Christianity, Islam, Buddhism, even atheism and agnosticism, that resonate in my being and in the face of the unknown revealing itself to me. It is a place in which I can celebrate the vast diversity of philosophical thought and religious experience but not rely upon it. This may be an uneasy, tentative place, but it can also be a secure and open one, perhaps only to myself.

My heart is now my refuge. Sensing a higher ignorance, I no longer bring the universe "into me." I bring myself "into it." When I do, I am inclined to believe that we are all connected to each other and the universe in ways we cannot fully imagine, only sense, inexplicably yet indelibly. The spiritual or mystical sense cannot be commanded, only nurtured to allow the possibility of "peeking" into the mystery of existence and our place within it. A profound sense of reverence and humility sweeps over me when I pause to embrace this prospect. Discovery now finds me, and I am no longer lost. My faith takes flight in the wonder of it all.

Believing

Another quiet, magical Christmas evening sweeps me away on the soft, gentle wind of hope. My mind is full of joyful memories and anticipation, alive in the enchantment of holiday traditions. I long to preserve the incredible joy of existence and meaning longer than is possible, I suppose. I wish the same for others. The sparkling lights of the Christmas tree, the haunting beauty of traditional music, and the scents of noble fir and plum pudding candles weave a spell on me. Something mystical closes in and hugs me.

There is no God, I suspect. No cosmic connection to our existence. No wondrous extension of life beyond death. I am deeply saddened by this prospect. My intellectual integrity allows no grand leap of faith nor does it offer a small measure of comfort. My being aches at the thought of extinction.

At times such as this, I search for space in my being to believe, if only tentatively for a moment, without embracing metaphysical presumptions. In this instance, I celebrate the simple and pure wish for foreverness, affirming the universe's miraculous gift of life, and believing that we can make a difference in adding hope and meaning to the human condition.

Love is all that matters.

For one magical moment, I willingly, even eagerly, suspend the critical, skeptical edges of my mind. It feels good. I give in to believing without reservation for several long, deep breaths. As I drift into this magical space, I more fully sense that my "beholding" of the universe is limited and myopic, and that I am "beheld" in some infinite, inexplicable manner by something greater, more wondrous, and more exquisite than I can imagine.

For one precious, holy moment, I believe again.

Final Truth

I don't know.

I don't know whether there is a God or not, nor do I possess sufficient reason or evidence for a belief or leap of faith that there is or not, so I am neither a theist nor an atheist. This assertion holds for any other metaphysical proposition.

I don't know whether it is possible to know or not, nor do I possess sufficient reason or evidence for a belief that it is impossible to know or not know whether there is a God, so I am not an agnostic.

I don't know whether it is possible to know, but absent other evidence, it is reasonable to assume that it may be. I acknowledge the possibility, however remote, that we may know or at least possess sufficient reason or evidence to form a belief in such a proposition. For lack of a descriptor, I am a hopeful skeptic.

I don't know if it is possible to obtain sufficient evidence to verify metaphysical propositions. It seems unlikely that credible (scientific) empirical evidence is possible. Such metaphysical propositions may exceed the limits of our current epistemological capacity or reach. It seems, however, that if we are willing to acknowledge that our view of reality is limited, then we must resist the notion that such metaphysical propositions, even if viewed as nonsensical, should be summarily dismissed.

I don't know if it is possible to develop alternative methods of discovery or "knowing" (e.g., mystical or spiritual) to verify metaphysical propositions. Such methods may not generate scientifically credible evidence, but they may or may not be sufficient in providing reason to form belief. If such methods lead to different beliefs, it is reasonable to assume that such beliefs lack credibility.

I don't know if it is possible to form a belief in metaphysical propositions that is reasonable and meaningful. At best, such beliefs are merely our "best guess" if formed rationally or our "fondest hope" if formed emotionally. They represent "leaps of faith." Assertions of knowledge are likely to be dogmatic and delusional.

I don't know if it is possible to hold such a metaphysical belief without compromising our cognitive ability to accurately observe what is, to accurately form perceptions, and to accurately construct reality.

In the end, the assertion that "I don't know" is all I do know regarding such metaphysical propositions. I do know that it is possible to live a meaningful life and not know or even believe in such ideas. We are part of the deep mystery around us. To me, this is final truth.

NOTE: The Buddhist perspective that metaphysical propositions are beyond our capacity to discover or know may be reasonable and wise. Rather than invest intellectual energy in such endeavors or to form beliefs about such, it seems best to suspend such efforts and concentrate on the promise of this life.

Vital Lies

There are lies we have to tell. We tell them because they make us feel good. They shield harsh reality and appeal to our deepest hopes and fears. They are easy to tell because most of us want them to be true. We hear them being told so vigorously all around us that we assume that they must be true. The lies sustain our mental health, generating less dissonance than the unsettling questions arising from the human condition.

It would be tempting to delineate these lies. I will not do so except for two universal ones. The first "vital lie" is that we may recognize a lie when we see it. We believe we can: it is any assertion incongruent with our point of view. However, we construct our reality with philosophical, economic, political, environmental, and religious beliefs, and we use labels to differentiate and reinforce our views. Once our "reality box" has been constructed, we don't want facts to interfere with the truth. It is much more comfortable to live with such lies, deny the effects, resist changes, and continue believing what we believe.

To confound the matter further, the effects are often difficult to discern, because they are gradual and constant. Place a frog in a boiling pot, and it will jump out, but place the frog in cold water and turn up the heat gradually, and you have a boiled frog. To avoid becoming a "boiled frog," critical thinking is essential, mindful of both sound arguments (based on logic and fact) and cognitive biases in the thinking process. That's a formidable challenge, which is why we may not know a lie when we see one.

The second lie is that if we recognize a lie, we will do something about it. Believing that we honor the truth not only tends to interfere with our ability to challenge it, it also interferes with our willingness to change our view of the truth even when we become aware of lies. We may be too weak to confront lies, too impotent to change, and too passive to care. Such lies may be like dreams from which we never wake. Vital lies. Vital for what?

In Praise of Doubt

I have heard the hopeful voice of theism,
   and *doubt* has been my companion,
      questioning unrelentingly…

      the presumptions of religious dogma,
      the enormity of human suffering and evil,
      the silence and impotency of God,
      the effects of faith and religious practice.

I have been drawn to the reasoned echo of atheism,
   and *doubt* has been my companion,
      questioning unrelentingly…

      the assumptions of negation and denial,
      the bounds of rationality and logic,
      our naïve sense of reality and purpose,
      the effects of persistent skepticism.

I have entertained the intellectual appeal of agnosticism,
   and *doubt* has been my companion,
      questioning unrelentingly…

the paradigmatic constraints of science,
the limits of our epistemological capacity,
the scope of the known and unknown,
the effects of intellectual resignation.

Doubt has been a trusted, life-long companion.

It has sought to protect me from untruth.

It has preserved my intellectual integrity and
sovereignty.

It has been kind in supporting my search for meaning.

It has nurtured a stronger faith in the wonder and
mystery of life.

It will embrace and sustain my last breath.

Blessing and Curse

My grandfather was a rational person, a self-proclaimed atheist, and a Marxist. He thought that people, exhausted by the human condition, searched for hope in God and that in the process, exonerated themselves from responsibility for the conditions of their existence. He believed that a good society created social justice, balancing the scales of rich and poor, educated and ignorant, strong and weak, healthy and disabled. He was an armchair philosopher of the first order, and I was his primary student.

Beneath this rational layer lurked something inexplicable: clairvoyance. He seemed to have this extraordinary gift tucked away in his inquisitive mind—seldom acknowledged, frequently denied, and discretely revealed only to those closest to him. It was unsettling because of its incongruence with his view of reality and an otherwise unfriendly, indeterminate universe. When talk of philosophy subsided, he talked about personal problems I shared with no one as if he were looking over my shoulder when they occurred. It seemed magical to me as a child, yet when I asked him how he knew these things, he smiled and said he just did.

My grandfather told me stories about our Hungarian heritage that seemed to linger quietly in the catacombs of his consciousness, of gypsies who danced around evening campfires, playing their stringed instruments, singing and laughing, and who foretold fortunes, read palms and cards, and gazed at crystal balls and candles. He said these clever inventions were designed to mask the underlying gift of vision. They could blame the fortune-telling cards or lifelines in palms for dark visions and avoid direct responsibility and hostility. His stories spoke of a long history of persecution, and families being torn apart, of hardships and suffering, and of constant migration to find a home. Gypsy history traces back to northern India, to Hindu origins, and to nomadic bands of roving circus performers who entertained others with stunts, tricks, and of course, magic. They migrated westward through Persia and Turkey, often settling in mountainous regions, later up the Danube River Valley into the fertile farm regions of Hungary. He told me of a great-grandfather who was born along the north shore of Turkey and of his Persian grandmother. He recounted family history in Central Europe and how his gypsy ancestors became intertwined with them. Pride abounded in his stories of love, toil, and sacrifice.

It may be impossible to discern between reality and myth, between history and fiction. Many of his stories have faded from my recollection, but the passion with which my grandfather told them flows in my veins today. He believed his gift allowed him to look back into the past and "experience" what happened. Images might resonate with clarity and detail, or they might be fleeting and oblique, most often rising unexpectedly and randomly. He considered this retrospective vision to be a *blessing* for the most part, because he could recount the history of his family, and come to know his ancestors. It seemed that there was much more than mere memory at play, something mystical and mysterious, taking him back in time to actually experience distant events. Sound and smell and taste resonated through his senses. He could not entirely control what flowed to him, but for the most part, he seemed to delight in it and was often overcome by a deep sense of gratitude for what his ancestors ultimately gave him.

When my grandfather foresaw unfortunate events, it troubled him deeply, and he viewed it as a *curse*. He did not want to know if something bad was going to occur, because he felt compelled to intervene or felt powerless and despondent. He resisted dark visions by attempting to distract himself. When he foresaw events, he occasionally shared them with me, holding my hands tightly. In those cases, however, the events that he foresaw were mostly positive. As I grew older, I suspected that the power of his personality influenced these outcomes and that his visions were guided by a desire to help family members. Perhaps with age and experience, his intellect nurtured wisdom and intuition, blended with imagination, and created a unique reconstruction of social reality. Surely, there was a rational explanation.

The universe may be far stranger than we can imagine. Why is there something rather than nothing? Why does it appear to be so peculiar? Our sense of reality seems myopic and our rationality seems bounded. Imagine that all human history, including every individual life, is indeed predetermined. Free will would be an illusion, masking hidden causation. In such a world, fate would be supreme and human choice irrelevant, for whatever we think or do would not affect the outcome. All of human development and motivation would be driven by forces beyond our cognizance and control. Some might assert that all is a dream in a cosmic imagination. However absurd, when a rational mind collides with the phenomenon of clairvoyance, it creates a seismic crack in the cosmic egg.

An Old Journal Entry

When my grandfather died, I regretted not being closer to him in my adult years. As he was eulogized, my mind drifted back to my childhood bond with him, all he taught me, the stories he shared, and the gift of vision he had. I wrote about his gift in my journal:

"A rapid stream of sunrises imploding into sunsets, hurries past tomorrow's shores with but momentary glimpses of humanity's new generation: inexplicable, yet intimate in their sense of meaning. The stream dries as it quickly envelopes my inner self, and vision flees. Rare discoveries remain: quiet pools settling in the abyss of consciousness, clear and illuminating in filtering a panorama of future into a second of time. A future strangely familiar, not growth's mere projection nor history's persistent encore, but a strata of eternity worn thin and smooth by the stream's rush to extinction. Here is a gift of my children's horizons behind me and their children's world before me."

I am unsure what to believe. Predetermination and precognition are inconceivable in my view of reality. My grandfather would agree, but in the end, he could not deny his vision. He didn't like it or want it, nor could he command it or explain it. A gift segued from one generation to the next, albeit to only a few. It is a wonderful mystery that gives me reason to pause with a profound sense of humility and reverence.

Uncommon sight is the legacy of my heritage.

Not to Worry

Existentialists tend to focus on the dark side of the human condition. Suffering and extinction are our ultimate fates. We shake our psyche with existential angst, for we cannot escape meaninglessness, helplessness, and nothingness.

This philosophical perspective, however, may yield liberation from delusion and denial and a subsequent realization that we alone are responsible for our lives and the form they take. Though confounded by life's complications, we remain sufficiently free to choose our lives and the people we become. Surely, there are limitations and boundaries to our being and its becoming, but we have the power to achieve much and overcome much, with or without God.

Existential encounters with the dark side of the human condition need not be foreboding. Seldom fear death; rather, regret its inevitability. Aging down the slippery slope of atrophy, the dark side may provide our imagination with a contrast in which the bright side is more illuminating and meaningful. Memories become more robust, fading less from mind's grasp when we embrace life and death authentically. Each day contains reason to pause and marvel at the beauty of existence. We may not appreciate each precious moment fully, but there are enough of them to allow us to celebrate life and its persistent wonder.

Fear of death is a natural but morbid nuisance. It seems more natural to endeavor to enjoy life fully with each breath and not dwell on its end. Even when bad moments and bad days haunt us, when we may be less than our best self, when we act in stupid and unkind ways, there is revelation in such moments, inviting us to make things right. We are unfinished. I could use less ego and a few more lifetimes to improve on my many faults and weaknesses.

It is good to muse about philosophy. It is a gift that we can give ourselves—enjoying our life as best as we possibly can, hoping to not mess up too many things. There is nothing to worry about as life ends; it is the way it is. Why not choose instead to worry about the life we live and love fully. Resist converting hope into delusion, choosing instead to temper such resistance with profound reverence for the unknown—a spark of religious faith, a small delightful delusion, or even an open mind.

There is no need to worry.

High School Reunion

Somewhat impulsively, true to "midlife crisis" form, a 1969 Datsun 1600 "rag top" Roadster found its way into my life. Red, of course. Driving it around the western Oregon countryside invited a sense of freedom and independence. It was a sunny-day toy for a middle-aged man. My wife, Linda, was embarrassed to see a father of teenagers act so silly. Other older men chase younger shadows, but not her husband. She viewed it as frivolous until one day, home alone without any other car, she had to drive it and fell in love instantly. She hid her smile at first. After that, the old roadster became a family member.

We decided to drive it to Linda's twentieth high school reunion in Olympia, Washington, some 240 miles away. Most of the route was on Interstate 5. The weather was perfect, or so it seemed. Halfway into the trip, the sky darkened, and it began to rain so hard that our Roadster's top was leaking. With no defrost and poor wipers, the old Roadster began to moan and groan. Without warning, the headlights and dash lights faded and dimmed. The car sputtered, and the engine stopped, leaving us along the side of a freeway in an unusually remote and dark area, with no sign of lights or life in the

Finding Heart

distance. The surprise storm intensified, obscuring our little car and its small reflectors as transport trucks sped by. It was a frightening predicament to say the least. Cell phones hadn't been invented yet. We were marooned.

We had no choice but to start walking to the nearest town for help. We walked two miles to the nearest freeway exit, but there was no sign of even a farmhouse, much less a service station. Still no lights in the distance. Cold and wet, we walked on. My wife said a prayer, followed by a smile when the rain let up. It was still dark and foreboding, and the next exit could not be seen in the distance, so we decided to hitchhike. I stuck out my thumb, but it was unnoticed in the darkness. Who would be willing to pick up two strangers in "the middle of nowhere, in the dark of the night"?

After a half-hour and our hope fading, a pickup truck pulled over. The guy was friendly and asked if that was "our little red car" back there. To our considerable surprise, he was heading to Olympia and had gone to Linda's high school. Amazing coincidences tend to prompt an annoying, faithful smile from my wife. We declined his offer to go to Olympia, but accepted a ride to the nearest service station. The first lights were in the little town of Kalama, and fortunately, the only service station was still open at 10:30 p.m. After calling for a tow truck, we headed back down the freeway to get our car. It sat there, battered by the storm, still and lifeless. Jump-starting it was of no avail, so we towed it to Kalama. The service attendant announced that he "knew nothing about cars," and the only auto repair shop in town was closed for the weekend. I enjoyed a skeptic's frown.

Not for long. The repair shop owner was called and agreed to come down to the station and look at our car. Another faithful smile. He arrived and gave the car a quick glance of dismay. We pushed it one block to his garage. He looked at it again and indicated that the problem was the distributor, the closest auto parts store was in Kelso, about thirty miles to the south, and it was closed on weekends. Worse yet, they probably didn't have such a part for an old foreign car. It would have to be ordered on Monday from Seattle, and our car would not likely be ready until the end of next week. No smile from Linda.

Stuck in Kalama, thoughts of an enjoyable high school reunion began to fade. The storm was worsening again. It was too late to call Linda's parents, as it was nearly midnight, and they were eighty miles away in Olympia. Fortunately, there was a motel in town. We took our luggage and walked in the downpour to the motel. Thoughts of a warm shower and a good night's sleep provided welcomed relief. As we entered the motel, we saw the desk clerk hand over the key to the last available room. No room at the inn. Sleeping in the car was out of the question, as it was locked up in the repair shop. The town was dark, the rain was hard, and the temperature was dropping. We were soaked and exhausted. Not our idea of a fun weekend.

We found a pay phone and looked through the yellow pages for ideas. Linda said another prayer, which was comforting to her but of no practical value to me. I waited for her standard response to emergencies: call a local branch of our church for help. There were no listings except for one in Longview, some twenty miles away. We called the number, hoping that someone might answer on a Friday night after midnight. To our surprise, a woman did answer. She listened to our plight, and indicated that a couple who attended the church lived in Kalama, so "try them." We did and explained our situation to the man who answered. His response was memorable: "I will be there in five minutes to get you." Amazing, given the fact that we were strangers to him. Linda smiled again. Faith can really be annoying to a rational man who is trying to cope with harsh realities.

We huddled in a closed restaurant doorway to keep warm. A car pulled up, and an older gentleman waved us in and introduced himself as Tom. I sat in front and Linda in back. His easy manner settled our concerns, and quick introductions and appreciation gave way to conversation as we drove up the hill to his home. "My wife is preparing some warm soup; you two must be cold and tired. We have a back bedroom where you will be comfortable." I reached over the seat to squeeze Linda's hand. "What seems to be the problem with your car?" he asked. The thought of warm soup and sleep quickly faded into reality's despair. I explained that we had a '69 Datsun Roadster and the distributor went out. The car slowed and he turned toward me to say, "Is that so? I own an auto parts store in Kelso, and if I'm not mistaken, I have what you need. We can get it in the morning." I could feel Linda's beaming, faithful smile on the back of my neck. I was speechless, so Linda responded graciously, "That's wonderful." She may have sensed that something mystical was peeking over the bounded edge of my rationality, and she tried to hide her delight over humbling a skeptic. Just maybe, God had found us "in the middle of nowhere, in the dark of the night."

At Tom's home, the hospitality was overwhelming. After a short visit and a good night's sleep, a pancake breakfast was waiting for us. It was fortunate that the older couple was in a position to help, as they were planning to retire "in the sun" and could have easily left the area already. They had been trying to sell their house for nine months, but not a single party was interested, as the town was small and not a place of attraction to outsiders. In spite of ample reason for discouragement, they were buoyant in their enthusiasm for life and transparent in their openness to complete strangers in need. After breakfast, we drove to town to look at our car. Lifting the hood, we discovered that the problem was a loose alternator belt. After exchanging a perturbed glance with the repair shop owner, Tom made the adjustment, and the car was drivable again. No need for a trip to Kelso. "Another miracle," Linda whispered. Hugs and thanks were exchanged warmly along with promises to return for a visit. The bond of genuine kindness was incredibly powerful. We drove off under a bright morning sun, just in time to reach Olympia for the reunion.

Reunions are always self-revelations, engaging strangers who were once friends. At the evening dinner dance, Linda was in her element, socializing easily, talking and dancing, remembering names at a bewildering pace, and exchanging hugs. I tagged along, shaking hands with blank faces, and listening to countless stories. Hours of music and conversation, within which lingered quiet moments filled with haunting flashbacks to Kalama.

We left Olympia early on Sunday evening, wanting to find a special gift for the couple in Kalama. Flowers, jellies, candy? Nothing seemed right. Perhaps a warm expression of appreciation was the best gift. Eighty miles later, we were driving up the hill to their home, and saw the For Sale sign for the first time. We also noticed "Sold" across it. The couple greeted us warmly when we arrived, and explained that shortly after we had left, a party came to see their house and made a cash offer. The couple was jubilant. They could retire now. Kindness repaid? Driving back down the hill, Linda's smile was replaced with tears. We both wept.

I offer no explanation, though it gives a skeptic reason to pause. For Linda, God had reached out to us through a very special couple in "the middle of nowhere, in the dark of the night."

In Praise of Hope

Ancient *hope*, not new faith,
rises in my being. It endures
from the dawn of humanity. It
is natural, whispering softly of
the things that matter most.

Hope beckons the magic of
existence, small miracles and
subtle wonders of life, willingly
suspending disbelief to allow a
space for faith to be nurtured.

It may be laced with delusion if
imagination and passion overwhelm
logic and reason. A higher ignorance
silences such concern, warming my
conversation with living things again.

Hope senses that there may be more
to effect than cause, more to mind than
consciousness, more to sense than
perception, more to the universe than
science reveals, more to me than imagined.

In my quiet moments, *hope* touches me profoundly. It revives a latent religiosity, never hostage to metaphysics. It yearns, even searches for any trace of purpose intimately connected to the universe.

Hope may be absorbed into my being from the unknown beyond my reach, uncreated. It wanders in wonder, never lost. It is my sentinel in the darkness, holding its torch high, never extinguished.

The sun will most surely set. *Hope* provides no answers and asks no questions. It just is. It celebrates my sunrises, this gift of life. It brightens my sunsets, allowing me to face the darkness with grace and reverence.

Bottles in My Cellar

(This prose is not a literal description of a physical cabinet. It is a metaphorical description of my mind.)

I have a collection of bottles in an old cabinet in my cellar, each a different size, shape, and hue. Each holds an intriguing blend of ingredients, thoughtfully selected to enhance the senses. Most bottles contain common ingredients, yet no one bottle contains all possible ingredients, and a few contain rare ingredients. I enjoy sampling the contents of each bottle to admire its color in the light, to inhale its unique aroma, and to savor its poignant taste. Each bottle invites me to taste life more fully. I bring each separately with me onto my balcony, drinking fully and raising it to the sun.

The cabinet containing these bottles is unlocked and available to others who may choose to sample them. I invite my friends to do so. The bottles have different labels familiar to most, but I only selected those that appeal to my palate, not a complete array. I understand that some of my friends prefer a particular bottle and choose to drink its content for most of their life. Others enjoy blends and stir the contents of various bottles into a single vat. When I have experimented with such formulas, I discovered that flavor and body were lost, so I prefer to enjoy the entire collection separately. I drink from all, at different times, in different ways. I take what I want or need from each and leave what I don't need.

The round, pale-orange bottle labeled "Buddhism" contains a drink with the aroma of mindfulness and loving kindness, the taste of being centered in the present, of setting aside metaphysics and authority, and the color of wildflowers in a high mountain meadow.

An elegantly shaped, purple bottle labeled "Existentialism" is another favorite. I drink it with French cheese and bread on my patio. Its aroma has the fragrance of free will and self-responsibility. It has the tart taste of stark reality, clearing my view of the human condition, and its dark color reflects little light or delusion. I avoid its taste on cloudy days, as it can be depressing.

"Music" is part of my art collection of bottles. It is a multicolored, exquisitely shaped bottle, large and at times cumbersome. Classical, rock, and jazz flow from its contents but only selections that lift my spirit or give me reason to dance. Its taste helps me to relax on a rainy day.

My "Health" bottle often gets shoved to the back of the cabinet, its pale-green hue fading into the shadows. Its nutritional drink tastes poorly at times, but it prevents excess weight and relieves retrospective guilt. My "Fitness" bottle, bright blue and shiny, is nearby. I have no trouble drinking of its contents daily, though its taste is of sweat, its aroma is unpleasant, and its color is bland.

One intriguing bottle is labeled "Wilderness." Its color reflects the hues of the mountains, seashore, and canyon lands. Its aroma is fresh air. Its taste is like clear, cold mountain stream water. It compels me to explore and discover, and to stretch myself beyond the comfortable. It can be intoxicating.

"Christianity" is an ivory-colored bottle with ingredients limited to the Catholicism of my youth and the Mormonism of early adulthood. It is a blend containing the virtues of education, hard work, and service to others. Some friends suggest that only one "Religion" bottle be in my cellar, but my home seems brighter when my cabinet is more inclusive. This bottle contains some rare spices from Hinduism, Confucianism, Islam, and Judaism.

"Critical Thinking" is a dark-red bottle with an array of contents. You need to shake it prior to tasting to ensure a balanced blend of analytic philosophy, cognitive psychology, and behavioral economics. Once tasted, my mind spins with clarity, mindful of biases that compromise sound thinking. Drinking too much, however, may invite napping on a rainy day.

I cannot begin to describe all of the bottles in my cabinet, as I am more interested in drinking discretely than in gurgling abstract descriptions. Some of the bottles are not nearly as full as they were earlier in my life, whereas others are brimming. Some bottles have been replaced with larger ones, but I save the original ones for purely sentimental reasons. A few have been discarded as my perspectives, interests, and values have changed. There is only so much room in the old cabinet.

A bright yellow bottle is labeled "Home." When I drink from it, I am overcome by a mystical sense of place, the natural world around me, and the wonder of living things within it. Next to it is my "Family" bottle, pale green and round in shape, with a few scars and blemishes. I drink from it to celebrate my heritage and my family: a good wife and amazing children and grandchildren.

The cabinet in which the bottles reside was built by my grandfather. He initially filled my bottles with ideas that he believed would help me in my life's journey. His inscription on the cabinet is *Philosophy*.

Each bottle alone is treasured and enjoyed. As I age, it becomes harder to get down the cellar stairs, so I keep a few bottles nearby. Toasting the setting sun, I drink slowly, savoring their taste and texture fully.

Reverences

Wilderness

 Traversing a high mountain ridge, the sweat on the back of my neck turns cold. A summer thunder storm is approaching, invading the tranquillity of warm sunshine, gentle breezes, and an azure sky. The wind is becoming stronger, the temperature is dropping, and curtains of rain appear in the distance. At times, mountains have their own temperament and create their own storms.

 My descent is steep and rapid. As I rappel down, the wind picks up, picks me up, a mere spider clinging to its web, its lifeline. Clouds are no longer above me but next to me, dark and foreboding. I sense the fury of nature within my bones, wild and untamed. Entering the forest below, I gaze back in homage, looking up through the mist. The mountain has disappeared, shrouded by the storm.

 I yearn for another day on the mountain to wander her meadows full of wildflowers and wildlife, to climb her steep ridges and glaciers, to stand on her summit with the rising and setting sun. Such thoughts have a sweet taste. Hiking out, I reflect on my time in the wilderness, and my aging body and spirit are renewed upon higher ground with vistas abounding. Here, mysteries of existence dance playfully around me. An inexplicable bond with the wilderness holds each of us, all of us as one.

When I return home, the world seems so confined. We move past each other unnoticed, immersed in the rigid patterns we made. Consumed by our own needs, an emotional storm approaches, cold and unforgiving. Families create their own temperament. Control overwhelms good sense. Different expectations generate conflict, as words become a harsh, bitter wind. Our silence and isolation lays our pain bare. Life's complications bewilder us. Our sanity becomes shrouded in the storm of personal conflict. Even after the storm passes, the wind is harsh and chilling.

My heart aches. We have known better times, moments of caring, touching one another. Here are smiles, tears, laughter, our deepest sorrow and greatest joy. I need to climb to higher ground above family discord, to inhale sweet, fresh air again. Sometimes, I lead the climb. Other times, I follow. I find unexpected kindness and understanding. I discover unspoken insights and affection. Love and compassion abound. The mysteries of being dance playfully around me. The intimate bonds of humanity hold me again, reminding me of what matters most in this life.

I enjoy wandering into the wilderness of nature, as it heightens my appreciation of the beauty and wonder in the world. I have also come to enjoy wandering into the "wilderness of humanity," as it holds the promise of finding heart. To the earth, the universe, and each other, we are intimately connected. Ancient cords deep in nature bind us all.

NOTE: Whenever I return from a sojourn in the wilderness, I read William Stafford's poem, "A Ritual We Read to Each Other." It provides reason to pause and seek higher ground in life.

On the Face

I can remember when I first
lifted my eyes, beheld the mountain,
and felt its reflection upon my face.

I cannot remember when I first
sensed the urge to climb, embracing
my being, moving me upward.

I cannot remember when I first
lost sight of the mountain, as I
hugged its face, held it close.

I cannot remember when I first
marveled at its majesty, the vastness
of all else, the nothingness of man.

I cannot remember when I first
saw the mountain's summit, as ridgelines
converged above me, and new vistas appeared.

I can remember when I first
stood on the summit, and held the rising
and setting sun in the palm of my hand.

I can remember.

(Climbing Mt. Rainier)

So Much Wonder and Beauty in the World

People ask me why I climb mountains, raft rivers, and spend so much time in the wilderness. The question is often accompanied by responses they rightly imagine: fresh air, pure water, natural habitat and wildlife, incredible scenery and terrain, star-filled night skies, perhaps some philosophical musing about nature, or the elusive search for mystical experiences. All of these reasons may be sufficient in and of themselves, yet there is much more.

There is little doubt that the wilderness astonishes us. It can be a retreat from the urban world in which we spend most of our time. It can renew us. However, that in itself is not its deepest revelation. The wilderness so separates me from my daily environment that I come to more fully appreciate the mostly unnoticed wonder and beauty around me. Every day, it teaches me profoundly. It lifts me to a higher level of perception, and to a deeper level of gratitude and humility.

It is a sad commentary on urban life when we have to escape into the natural environment beyond our cities, believing that it alone holds the promise of wonder and beauty. Certainly, we recognize the extraordinary in our otherwise ordinary existence. New life is one such miracle. Hearing the pulse of life within your partner's body is amazing, as are the first sounds of life in the delivery of a child and the first events of recognition, speech, walking, and personality. Another wonder is to stand in the presence of new love and union, the amazing bond of affection and commitment, as friends join their lives for a shared future. Being immersed in the arts also affords many wondrous moments in which the spirit is uplifted and beheld by music, artwork, or theater. The sciences also contain incredible discoveries that produce insights along the edges of the unknown, stirring our imagination. Such "big bangs" of life are all around us, and their meaningfulness is woven deeply into the human condition.

When our senses become dulled and ragged by the relentless press of daily existence, an escape to the wilderness provides opportunities for reflection and rejuvenation. As we enter the wilderness, we are conditioned to seek the "big bangs" of nature—incredible sunrises and sunsets, beautiful scenery and vistas, wild flowers and wildlife in amazing color and variety, and clear, star-filled skies. Because such wonders may not occur with sufficient frequency and vibrancy to stimulate the incurious mind, some people may find the wilderness barren and boring. We can find much more. In a desolate canyon landscape, life finds a way to persist, and it is fascinating to discover it. On high mountain ridges, deep river canyons, or intricate coral reefs, a closer inspection reveals wonder and beauty in abundance.

When alone in the wilderness, nothing speaks to me so clearly as what comes out of silence. It is never dark or empty. Rather, the silence is amazingly resonant and resplendent. As I hike up the butte behind my home in the

A Beautiful Mountain Range and Valley

morning, it is breathtaking to watch the play of sunlight and shadow through the forest, with the wind moving both around. It is fascinating to look beyond the surface of the forest, to find life beneath the ferns and underbrush, in the bark of old growth firs and cedars, in the touch of cool springs, in the taste of wild berries, in the fragrances dancing in the breeze. There is more going on in the natural world that is not captured in the net of our superficial observation, so I actively seek those "small sparks" of awe.

When I return from the wilderness, I see the intricate variety of life more clearly. It is not my vision of the wilderness that is so transforming but its effect on my daily view of the world. It teaches me to pause and observe the extraordinary all around me every day of my life. Observing two people feel each other's pain and extend themselves to help one another, sacrificing personally, is uplifting. Teaching my university classes to eager, young minds, only to receive more from them, is inspiring. During a rainy night walk with my oldest daughter through her neighborhood, delighting in the warm glow of homes and families, her glow is magical. Watching my son's tender patience and rich perspective in dealing with complications in this life is wondrous to me. On my knees next to my youngest daughter as we plant flowers in her garden, beholding the grace of her touch, is miraculous. Sharing memories, dreams, tears, and laughter with my life companion is fulfilling and beautiful. Moments, easy to miss, easy to forget.

The wilderness teaches further. As I become intimate with the earth and all living things, I become more capable of intimacy with others. As I recognize the "small sparks" of wonder and awe in the wilderness, I not only recognize their presence in my daily life, but I become more capable of creating such sparks, original and inarticulate, in my relations with others. As I give into the flow of this transformation, I discover that the emergence of these gifts is not random or rare but miraculously vibrant and abundant.

When my sense of the extraordinary in the ordinary begins to diminish, a yearning to wander in the wilderness, to anchor my being in what truly matters, arises again.

Tribute

We stand alone, silently, reverently, gratefully
in tribute to the grandeur of mother earth.

Just as we cradle the sparrow with tender wings,
she holds us in the palm of her gentle hand, and
lifts us to the wind to take flight and soar.

We, too, must hold her in our gentle arms,
protect and comfort her with delicate grace,
with purpose beyond our narrow interests.

We have been unkind to her, stripping her
substance, damaging her well being. Her pain
becomes our pain, even our loss forever.

We stand together, this day, defiantly, irreverently,
in sacred tribute to the grandeur of mother earth.

She has been our guardian.
May we have the wisdom to be hers.

Is It Over?

 The sweet scent of anise dances in the ocean breeze, the sounds of wind chimes fill the silence between crashing waves, and the sun plays hide and seek behind an endless flow of clouds as I explore the coastal wetlands, with my six-year-old grandson in hand. We pause to allow our senses to drink it all in—a moment raptured into beauty, then gone forever.

 Developing in my grandchildren an early appreciation for nature, for the earth and its environment, has become a growing passion. On a bluff high above the beach, we sit, and I say, "Close your eyes, and let the pure ocean air fill your lungs. What do you smell?" A deep breath and a deeper pause. "It smells like licorice, Grandpa." I point to the long, slender stalks of anise swaying nearby, and he rubs his fingers on its aromatic blossom. Allowing a moment for the bright-eyed discovery to sink in, I say, "Close your eyes and listen to the sounds around you. What do you hear?" A long moment. "I hear the waves crashing to shore, the wind passing through the tall grass, the sea gulls above and below us, and the sound of people on the beach. Lots of things, Grandpa." Nature is a symphony, I point out, that fills our senses with musical wonder. "Can you sense the silence, too?" I ask. "Yes, it is very quiet." He responds quickly, as if the question could not hold his active mind. It is an amazing stillness, the emptiness without sound, the space in which we can listen to our heart beat. "Now, look all around you, look beyond the things most people see. What do you see?" His gaze turns up and down the beach, his eyes widening. "I see the tide go out and shells appear on the sand, the seagulls glide and stand still in the wind, and a distant boat disappearing beneath the waves." I encourage him to look at the dazzling formations of clouds and imagine wondrous things: animals, flowers, almost anything. He lies on his back and stares at the sky, pointing as he imagines. He is beginning to touch the natural world around him.

We walk down to the beach and climb over the rocks, discovering sea life in abundance: starfish, mussels, crabs, and small fish in tide pools. His mind is a sponge, absorbing all I can give and more. Our senses vibrate in this magical place, free from urban distraction, and the fibers of our being connect with the earth. Here are moments of contemplation and relaxation, of mindfulness and thoughtlessness, of possibilities and peace.

Daylight lingers as the sun touches the western horizon, spreading pink and purple hues across the sky. We can see the universe opening its infinite canopy of stars to the east. Another day is fading away. We sit quietly to enjoy the exquisite embrace of nature, reaching out to hug and hold us. Sitting close, my grandson lifts his serious eyes to meet mine and asks, "When we die, is it over?" Such a question for a six-year-old. Simple. Natural. Far reaching. My being is suspended in the moment, frozen by the uncertainty that has haunted humanity since the dawn of time and thought. The face of innocent curiosity awaits my response like a bud in springtime, longing for the taste of morning rain, for the touch of afternoon sun.

Nearly thirty years ago, my six-year-old daughter asked a similar question, wondering if our family would be together forever. My response was framed in ambiguous rhetoric, affirming her belief in angels and heaven, and my belief in much less, seeking to preserve her innocence and my integrity, I thought. Without the mention of metaphysics, I assured her that we would be but in what way was a conversation for a later day. Now, as my grandson inquires, I wonder if a response is possible, if it outreaches human imagination, much less knowledge, or if it is closer, so intimate that our best philosophy is impotent in the face of it. Ultimately, the deepest mysteries of life, in all their splendor and wonder, may elude discernment.

Sitting quietly, contemplatively, with eyes fixed on me, my grandson waits for my response. My words come slowly and deliberately. "We hope it's not over, but we don't know for sure. There are a lot of different ideas about what happens."

I search for the right words, concerned about shattering his gentle innocence, cluttering his young mind with metaphysics, and yet preserving hope and possibility. I point out that such answers are best found in nature and that most of us spend a lifetime looking for them, each discovering our own answers, just as he finds shells in the sand. His mind is searching, reaching just as the waves reach toward shore.

He looks at me with puzzlement. "Grandpa, when you die, will I see you again?" In the presence of a child's pure innocence, unconcerned about God and heaven, only about whether we will continue to be together, a wave of humility overcomes me. That is what matters most to him. "I sure hope so, but that's a long time away." "I will miss you when you die, Grandpa." "I know you will. I will miss you, too, but imagine that I will be watching all of the wonderful things you will do in your life." With reassured eyes, he smiles and seems to understand.

Existential wonder is woven into the fabric of our existence, with each curvature of space and each flux of time, inexplicably and indelibly connecting our consciousness with the universe at a higher level of being. It taunts our deepest imagination, strains our best science, and exposes the naiveté of our best philosophy, our most eloquent poetry, and our most insightful religion. In the end, all such musing is obliterated by a child's simple, searching question, one for which there is no concrete answer. I hug him closely and tell him that even his grandfather cannot answer all of his questions, that he needs to continue to search, to ask questions and question answers, and that if he is patient and persistent, he will find answers in time.

Inhaling the ocean air deeply, I feel love for my grandson and hope in his promise. This simple hope reveals that life is precious, love matters more than belief, meaning is more important than truth, and unlike truth, we create it in all we are.

The stars are holding us now, spreading endlessly across the clear night sky, this infinite ocean above and beyond us. The distant lighthouse shines its beacon to ships at sea. I tell him to imagine out there, somewhere, a single star that is ours alone, and like the lighthouse, it is a beacon that guides us. "I think that one is mine, Grandpa." He points to a bright star low on the western horizon. He smiles and drifts off to sleep. I carry him on my back up the beach, another day behind us.

It is over.

(At Cannon Beach on the northern Oregon coast)

Strangers

How easily some people come together, quickly detecting a spark of lasting affinity in the pulse of our common humanity. Even differences bind us.

A moment is shared. We are connected, enriched in this easy exchange. Conversation with dreams and feelings is enjoyed, and so much more, unspoken.

Are we strangers? A hint of distant yesterdays haunts us when we may have met. The only strangeness rests in the inexplicable, yet natural closeness leaping out of our being.

Her Touch

My oldest daughter came home today. She helped me with autumn thinning, winter memories, and springtime visions of the beauty to come.

I watched her closely. Her touch was delicate. She pruned the living plants to nurture future growth, providing ample space and light, and she removed the dead plants completely. Their time had come and gone. Her pace was steady and her mood upbeat. She was a gardener in the midst of furthering life's cycle, looking to a new day of sunshine and blossoms. Every time our eyes met, there was a smile and easy conversation. A quiet sorrow that nature has her way was unspoken.

I reminisced as fathers are prone to do when adult children return home. There were reflections of her childhood, our togetherness, spending time in the garden, loving her flowers, and later drawing them in her artwork—stories her father could tell as if they occurred but yesterday, vivid and brimming with colorful detail. Fathers have the advantage of inciting the humor and joy around those haunting moments.

After finishing our gardening, we retreated to the little cabin down the hill. She graciously listened to my musings as I shared a poem or two to connect us in the soil of life's garden. One poem connected us with my mother, speaking of flowers and springtime, of hopefulness at the end of winter, our ending. No words were spoken, just a soft smile and warm hug, giving a gift of comfort to me, her father, and a springtime vision in her gentle embrace.

If hope beyond death is in vain, I can rest and close my eyes with a final breath, knowing that the beauty of the garden will endure, entwined in the lives of my loved ones. Just as seeds of plants sustain new growth, some lingering trace of me will remain with my family, not a mere memory, but my presence will continue to touch them in the quiet hours of their lives. Somehow, I will know of their blossom, because I will be a part of it, even if my touch is unnoticed. A gift of vision only a loving daughter can give.

We walked around the property, hand in hand. I showed her what I had done to the land, and I shared what this place had done to me. The grass seemed so green, the sky so blue, the sun so warm, and the air so pure. The breeze filled her hair, and she smiled, laughing with me. I felt so incredibly blessed to have her in my life—my little girl, this amazing woman.

At Play

I watch my son and smile as we wander along the stream in the wooded area behind his home in Colorado. In his youth, he would not allow us to force God into him. Something deep within him resisted. Much more than adolescent rebellion, he defiantly proclaimed his atheism in those early days, recoiling at the religious nonsense around him.

Later in life, I noticed that his time in the wilderness led to a subtle shift in perspective and philosophy. He told me of his hikes in mountains, forests, and canyon lands, and he spoke of the natural world around him, reaching out to him. He described swirling columns of leaves rising almost magically from the earth, sensing something mystical was at play. He immersed himself in the stars at night. He was completely alive in the wilderness, at home finally.

Now, I watch him again. There is a profound reverence in him for the mystery, wonder, and miracle of life rising out of the universe. He celebrates light rising out of darkness, beauty rising out of the light, and something incredible and sustaining rising out of nature. Maybe he has found his way to God, though there is little need for rationality to require much more.

As we wander, the child in him comes out to play. So full of joy and risk and energy. He plays with his children, balancing himself on logs, climbing trees, and skipping rocks in the stream. His laughter is easy. At times, I notice that he pauses and becomes quiet. He pays homage to nature around him, in him, drinking it in. Raising his arms, he would say to his mother: "This is my church."

The agnostic and atheist have faded in his consciousness, rarely raising their skeptical voices. He doesn't seem to pay attention to them anymore. There is peace in him and a willing suspension of disbelief in favor of the haunting mysteries of nature. His prayers are silent and inarticulate, unnoticed in the ebb and flow of his being. Faith in all that is, authentic and compelling in its presence, abides in him now.

I watch him and smile, my little boy, this beautiful man.

Her Way Alone

It is hard for me to imagine that my littlest girl is turning forty. She seems to be a unique soul finding her own way on life's incredible journey, older now but always young to me, always "my littlest girl."

Several years ago, she coped with divorce and relocation. She returned home to Eugene with her two young children. Though her resources were limited, her resolve was extraordinary, as were her imagination and artistry.

We found a small, run-down house in a quiet neighborhood for an affordable price. It was hard to imagine that anything in the house could be salvaged. No worry. The house was completely remodeled in seven weeks with lots of paint and hard work and love. It was a total family effort with her children, sister, brother-in-law, a few contractors, her mother and me.

How do you convert a house into a *home*? A flower garden was planted, enclosed by new lawn, shrubs, and fence. Her imagination held a simple vision: the beauty of nature outside gave way to the beauty of artistry inside. She had provided her children with a *home*.

She surprises, delights, lives simply, and finds happiness in many small and ordinary things. Working for hours in her flower garden, she brings enduring beauty to her home and to the lives of her children and all who enter. She redecorates, paints, and pays attention to the tiny details enhancing beauty. She embraces things that most of us take for granted, transforming the ordinary into the extraordinary. For her, it is simply what it is, nothing more.

In all of her creations, she pauses to bring others into her perspective so they can behold what she sees, and appreciate subtle changes transcending into beauty. In that exquisite encounter, an intimate bond with our environment is created as well, a bond which strengthens the well-being of her family.

She always has a way of teaching me more than I teach her: my littlest girl, this purely delightful woman.

Flowering

Cutting fresh flowers in a muddy
field under a gloomy, grey sky
was her early morning wish.

As I watched her, she would lift
each flower to an imagined sun,
and give praise for its beauty.

It was an unconscious ritual,
yet consecrated with a smile,
and a perfectly happy heart.

Returning home, stems were
re-cut, admired, and placed in
vases, lined across the counter.

Her pace was easy and graceful,
as each bouquet combined color
and shape, with her artistic touch.

Dancing about, she placed each vase
in the perfect place to reflect light and
fragrance, bringing beauty to our home.

Today, alone, as I enter each room,
her flowers greet me, hold me.
There is brightness, joy, and her.

Wandering Around on an Ordinary Day

Wandering around today, I am relaxing and drinking in the beauty of this place. Got up at dawn to do a few chores, opened the windows to drink in fresh air, and slipped back into bed, sleeping so late that the morning was nearly gone. I went to Saturday Market, ate good food, and listened to good music, in earthy, Eugene hippie style. The energy of the market seemed to hold me, invigorate me.

Walking down to the Willamette River, I stop by the classic auto center to check out new arrivals. A sweet, completely restored, old English sports car sold a few weeks back, and it would have tempted me to impulsive irrationality and expensive future repairs. Not a smart idea, but what fantasies are? I stopped to buy some shorts as the sun was warming up and so were my jeans.

As I wait for a long freight train to pass, I sit down by a couple of kids from San Diego on their way north, hoping for a chance to hop on a freight car. Free spirits seeking some springtime adventure and fresh memories. We laugh, talking about the places they have been and the ones we have in common. I imagine old, bearded Walt getting off a freight car and joining the conversation, commenting:

Great is youth, and equally great is old age....great are the
    day and night;
Youth large lusty and loving....youth full of grace and
    force and fascination,
Do you know that old age may come after you with equal
    grace and force and fascination?
Day full-blown and splendid....day of the immense sun,
    and action and ambition and laughter,
The night follows close, with millions of suns, and sleep
    and restoring darkness.
(Walt Whitman from *Leaves of Grass*)

The kids look at each other in a daze, wondering what
nonsense this old guy is uttering. With a spurt, they are up and
on the train, waving goodbye. Walt and I smile as he moves
on, too.

Stopping by the Skinner Butte rock columns to watch
climbers, I enjoy memories of climbing, some twenty years
distant. My old, aching body stretches in the sun, merely a
spectator. A young woman and her partner offer me a bottle of
water. Good conversation around our climbing stories. I wonder
what adventures are still possible and dream about buying a
round-the-world airline ticket and taking off for the summer.
Dreams are wonderful, inviting the imagination to be playful
and vibrant. I move on, wandering toward the river, north of
me. I imagine James sitting on the river's bank, commenting:

Walk easy on the earth:
    Each life has its own fragile rhythm,
    To be aware of it is to understand,
    To ignore it is abandon oneself to sadness,
    It is to search vainly for the wholeness
        that only comes in surrender to what is.
(James Kavanaugh from *Walk Easy on the Earth*)

James has a good way of cutting to the core. Most poets do. He gives me reason to pause and dream again.

I wander close to the river, hoping to witness springtime's new arrivals. Most of the ducks are safely tucked into the Delta Ponds, but nature is full of surprises. I find a blue heron's nest with two newborns, barely moving around. Their mother is not happy with my presence, even though they are well into the thick blackberry bushes. New life holds much promise, and nature always finds a way to persist and surprise us.

When I stop at a bench by the rose garden, I watch the river flow by. The current seems to cut deep within me. I am not alone, for I imagine William joining me on the bench. His presence is no surprise. After all, springtime is a time for poets to sing and philosophers to dance. He shares his soul with me:

> Sometime when the river is ice ask me
> mistakes I have made. Ask me whether
> what I have done is my life. Others
> have come in their slow way into
> my thought, and some have tired to help
> or to hurt: ask me what difference
> their strongest love or hate has made.
>
> I will listen to what you say.
> You and I can turn and look
> at the silent river and wait. We know
> the current is there, hidden; and there
> are comings and goings from miles away
> that hold the stillness exactly before us.
> What the river says, that is what I say.
> (William Stafford from *Ask Me*)

William is right. There is an intimate authenticity here, a clear wellspring of consciousness percolating into our presence, into our sense of well-being.

I wander farther downstream to find a secluded spot on the lawn above the river. Lying on my back, I marvel at the intricate play of shadow and light around me, changing constantly as the sun and clouds move by and the breeze moves living things around. Something mystical whispers to me quietly in all that is. The sunshine is not nearly as warm on my face as it used to be, and the cold of the shadow is more intense and dark. Life may be fading a bit in my being. I am fine until I imagine Dylan walking by, musing with depressing prose:

> Do not go gentle into that good night,
>   Old age should burn and rage at the close of day;
> Rage, rage against the dying of the light.
>   (Dylan Thomas)

Relax, Dylan, for I find no need for rage, much less for fear. The fading of the light is nature's way, and my being has been a miracle in itself. I find that there is much more reason to pause and celebrate the goodness and grace of life as the sun warms my face. When my time comes, I will go in peace and gratitude. In spite of my skepticism, I will go with a sense of wonder and awe, embracing reverence for life and its profound mystery. Dylan shakes his head in dismay and moves on upstream in search of God, perhaps.

I rise with a few aches and walk back along the bike path. Young people are riding their bikes. Children are playing in the park. An old friend and his wife run by, stopping for catch-up conversation and rekindled friendship. Even if I could, my old knees would not permit running again, but I am happy for them. Out here wandering around, even in the parks of a city far from the wilderness, I sense the beauty of humanity and nature and the intimate bond between them. I enjoy the birds' songs from the trees, the butterflies floating on the wind with the fragrance of flowers, and the dampness in the grass, for it speaks of life and its goodness. I think my thoughts freely. I breathe the sweet, pure air, and I am fully alive, wandering on this day and enjoying my presence in the presence of all that is. I imagine Ralph biking by, shouting his annoying refrain:

> There is no great and no small
> To the Soul that maketh all:
> And where it cometh, all things are;
> And it cometh everywhere.
> I am owner of the sphere,
> Of the seven stars and the solar year,
> Of Caesar's hand, and Plato's brain,
> Of Lord Christ's heart, and Shakespeare's strain.
>   (Ralph Waldo Emerson from *History*)

Okay, Ralph. I guess I needed that for some reason. Cause for reflection again.

I will live to wander another day. It may be across the planet or up the hill behind the home that centers my being. As I wander, my dreams and memories will sustain me in the sunset of life. As I wander down the river, William greets me again and puts his arm around me:

> I like to live in the sound of water,
> in the feel of mountain air. A sharp
> reminder hits me: this world still is alive;
> it stretches out there shivering toward its own
> creation, and I'm part of it. Even my breathing
> enters into this elaborate give-and-take,

this bowing to sun and moon, day or night,
winter, summer, storm, still – this tranquil
chaos that seems to be going somewhere.
This wilderness with a great peacefulness in it.
This motionless turmoil, this everything dance.
    (William Stafford from *Time for Serenity, Anyone?*)

I give a simple nod of appreciation as William wanders off. No words are spoken as our parting glance reveals a bond with the natural world.

I yearn to wander more often. Life is good, especially in the company of my old friends who sustain me. I find solace in their words. As I turn homeward, I find a note in my pocket from my old friend, Franz, and it captures my wandering heart.

I would be like trees are
with the river,
drink of you far below the surface of your flowing,
stand as they stand, my arms to the sunlight,
lost in your siren song
I would wait for storms of you
to cut away the earth and tell my story.
    (Franz Dolp from *Rivers: Reflections On The Infinite*)

It is good to wander around on an ordinary day.

(Along the Willamette River in Eugene, Oregon)

On Poetry

Poetry is pure reflection in
our romance with life, expressed
uniquely, fully, to sense meaning
from the unnoticed past and
present retreating from us.

It searches for fresh insight
and vision to enhance our
reality. Affinity with ultimacy
and intimacy endears us to
all of which we are part.

And so I write and rewrite. If
these are my words alone, then
I hope for understanding, and if
they are yours also, I hope we can
share that which is deepest in us.

At the Beach

Early morning, lying in bed, I hear the surf beckon me, lifting me from a dreamless sleep into a new day. I refuse to open my eyes and stretch my less-than-fully-rested body, but the sound of the ocean is persistent in its call. The tide is out. I, too, am swept out on the beach before breakfast with my grandchildren, searching for unbroken shells. Incoming waves cool my feet, and the rising sun warms my face. Here is another clear, beautiful day to catch the play of nature and life.

Time seems to slow at the beach. I see my grandchildren playing in the sand, building their castles and forts. Their mothers keep them close, mindful of the unpredictably powerful ocean before us. Never mind, there are waves to catch and rocks to climb, so I invite them to join me, promising to hold their hands tightly. I cautiously break the promise, and encourage them to explore and play. We draw pictures and mazes in the wet sand. They run after seagulls. We fly our dragon kite with its colorful tail so high. Their glee is tasteful to my soul. Precious spirits, spontaneous and untiring in easy laughter and daring, may our touch be gentle and kind.

I wish that every moment could be preserved. I wish that we could live forever. I wish that I could watch their entire lives unfold. Wishes carried away on the ocean breeze, fleeting.

It seems that you never tire of the beach. Something in the wind, sunshine, and ocean sustains us further, to the core of our being. We play in the waves, screaming at our frigid insanity. We lay in the sun as salt and sand cover our bodies. We walk along the shore, inhaling the fresh air. Something magical, mystical, and wondrous embraces us. I feel as if I can live forever. Maybe revelations are hidden in the sand or beneath the waves, playing with our fondest wishes.

The sun sails across the sky, and it is now touching the western horizon. Another day is slipping away, another beautiful gift of nature. We build a fire, roast marshmallows, and make s'mores. We tell nearly true stories, sing songs poorly, and laugh at the comedy of it all until there is no trace of sunlight. The fire dims into ambers, and my family dims into exhaustion, retreating to the beach house for the night.

I stay behind to relax and muse, gazing at fires up and down the beach, alone in my beach chair. The immense, impenetrable darkness closes in around me. I can hear only the crashing waves in the distance. So very alone. Nearly extinct, it seems. I wonder if there is a God out there, hidden in some distant galaxy or maybe nearby in the shadows along the beach. I wonder what life has yet to bring and what I have yet to give before this deepening void carries me away on its outgoing tide. When I ponder why there is something rather than nothing, I wonder why there couldn't be something more to us rather than nothing. Ultimately, life is a sweet mystery, compelling in its hopeful seduction.

As I close my eyes, my senses resonate and my reflections deepen. I am swept away by the memories of the day with my family at the beach. Love abounds. Life flourishes.

I look up and am comforted by this exquisite moment. Stars spread across the clear night sky, like sand along an infinite shore. The fire is out, and so is the tide. I rise and walk toward the ocean, unable to see my feet below me. I move slowly into the deepening darkness. I am invited, beheld by an abundant wonder. The universe is my companion.

As I approach the ocean, the flat beach stretches before me, and I see even more stars glimmering above. I stand in utter amazement as the vast universe reveals itself to me. As I walk, I look down, transfixed. The retreating ocean has left behind thin, wide sheets of water, precisely mirroring the stars above. No moon, clouds, or wind to distort reflection. Sky and beach merge into a cosmic whole of which I am an intimate part. Stars are everywhere, above me and below me, enveloping me. I traverse the Milky Way galaxy, millions of light years in each step. Here is peace, connecting me with all that is. I am completely alive. I am one with all that is.

I wonder if I am awake or dreaming. I wonder if I hear music in the wind and surf. The air is sweet and pure. I dance among the stars. Not alone. Not ever.

Infinite Shore

Many have walked before
along this isolated beach, some
with carefree spontaneity, others
with hurried desperation, each
building their castles,
dreaming their dreams,
leaving their footprints
in the sand.

All disappear, washed away
by the outgoing tide, yet beheld,
drifting upon the ocean's surface,
glimmering in the setting sun, and
in the beckoning darkness, rising
as stars with infinite variety, wonder
in the clear, night sky.

Realizations

Every Breath Is a Miracle

Every day I am alive is a miracle.

Every morning I awake to the warmth of sunshine or the soft fall of rain…

Every breath I take in the heights of joy or the depths of sorrow…

Every time I open my eyes to the radiance of a rainbow or the deep shadows of a forest …

Every sound I hear from songbirds in the morning or the wind moving trees around at night…

Every fragrance I inhale of the sweet scents of springtime or the crisp decay of autumn leaves…

Every word I speak of faithful promise or existential angst…

Every step I take in the exuberance of youth or the memorable aches of age…

Every evening I live in the embrace of a sunset or in the darkness of a storm…

I seek and find heart in the abundance of small, unnoticed miracles, slipping past quietly, forever present.

The touch of a loved one…

The courage to overcome loss…

The deepest and darkest suffering…

The gratitude of service to others…

The compassion arising toward others…

The most inspiring purpose imaginable…

Such gifts are miracles to all of us.

Not from a friendly universe. Not from a loving God. Not for any reason at all.

Only from what is. From what can be. From life itself.

Even a miracle when someone reads these words and celebrates with me.

Romancing Reincarnation

With age comes philosophical reflection about life: high peaks and low valleys along the journey, the comedy and tragedy, the overriding meaningfulness or senselessness of it all. In such reflection, it is tempting to fantasize about living life over again, to contemplate the things we would do differently, and to even provide some well-deserved applause or much deserved flogging.

I muse about living my life over again. It is a joyful romance with mysticism.

I would…

> enjoy nature more frequently and fully, even the wind in the trees and the sunshine or rain shower on my face,
> grow more flowers and inhale their fragrance and beauty more often, leaving them uncut in the garden and wild,
> mow the lawn less and walk barefoot on it, even in the rain, touching the living things with which I share this earth,
> sleep outside under the stars on moonless nights regularly, allowing the magic to sweep me away,

lie in my hammock, even in the winter, to listen to the natural world around me, to feel its pulse flow through me, become me,

seek adventure and discovery in more distant places, enjoying the people of the world more fully,

climb more remote mountains and raft more wild rivers, revering my connection with nature more completely.

I would…

love more completely,
sing and dance more freely,
laugh and hug more fully,
think less and feel more deeply,
be less safe and take more risks,
let people know they matter to me,
treasure and nurture lasting friendships,
seek authenticity and intimacy in every touch,
feel others' pain and joy more personally,
listen more actively and be still more often,
ponder the things that matter the most, and not be
    at the mercy of the things that matter the least.

I would…

take only what I need and share the rest,
accumulate less stuff,
travel light,
walk more gently upon the earth,
drink in more and miss less,
celebrate goodness wherever I discover it,
regret less and forgive more,

control less and cherish chaos more,
remain humble and acknowledge my ignorance,
be generous with greater kindness,
make a difference in the causes I serve,
live simply.

I would…

behold the wonder and beauty around me,
and allow myself to be beheld by it,
deeply, completely.

Life is too short for one lifetime.
I want one or two more,
somewhere, somehow, sometime.
But I cannot.
I don't believe it is possible.
I suspect you don't either.

Hope is a good thing, maybe the best of things,
for I may be wrong.
Our ignorance far exceeds our knowledge of the universe, and
our imagination is less robust than the deep mysteries
dancing playfully around us every day.
The darkness may hold a few surprises,
and this old skeptic is eager to find out.

But not too eager.
Not yet.
I love this life.
I love its richness and texture.
I love its warmth and vitality.

I even love its pain and heartaches,
    its complications and imperfections.
When I seek and find heart, I feel more fully alive, more
    insightfully human, more real and lasting.

So, I will live my final years as fully as possible.
I will cherish the sweet gift of existence with every breath.
I will hold the torch high to push back the darkness.
I will love as best as I can for as long as I can.

(Jefferson Park, Oregon)

Smiling at the Darkness

 I wonder if we may have lived before this life. Moreover, I wonder if there is a connection between our personalities as human beings and other living things. Imagination transcends any rationality lingering in such musing. It seems apparent that my life partner was a butterfly. Its life is a burst of beauty, spontaneous in flight, oblivious to direction, full of energy and color among the flowers and weeds, a pure joy to watch, and less imagined, a pure joy to live in this manner. I wonder to where or what she would transmigrate in her next life.

 As far as myself, my imagination is wanting for some idea of a prior life, but I don't have to look far to find a desirable next life. I opt to be a Golden Retriever, like my dog Luke. He eats great food, naps as much as he wishes, chases tennis balls for exercise, and looks so adorable with his big brown eyes that people cannot resist him. He is an inspiring role model, unconditional in his love and devotion. What a life, albeit a bit short. No intellect to weigh me down. I might even learn to relax. No bills or need to generate income; I might learn to live more simply. No stuff; I might learn that I don't need it. Of course, I would prefer to not be neutered. It's almost beginning to sound good to move to my next life. I might even learn that life can be good all by itself.

Best Gifts

Sometimes, the best gifts of life are among the last ones we are fortunate enough to receive.

My companion is an incredible woman, full of life, love, kindness, and compassion, so much so that her reach extends beyond our family to countless others. I have always loved her, though not always well. Sharp differences have separated us, the burden of which we jointly shared. With age, time, and wisdom, we have closed the gap in ways unexpected and unimagined.

She has given me an amazing gift in our later years. She has sought to understand me fully. She has actively listened to my philosophical musings, and read my writings with a more sensitive embrace. In turn, I have listened to her deepest reflections. In doing so, I have seen her clearly, beheld her fully, perhaps for the first time, and loved her completely, enjoying the delightful play of her being with mine.

Sometimes, the best gifts of life are among the last ones we are fortunate enough to receive.

A Final Thought

Finding heart along our life's journey is nourishing and meaningful. You have read my stories, essays, and prose. I hope that some of them resonate in your being, connecting you to the things that matter most.

As I share my stories with family and friends and they share theirs with me, I realize that while the context of my personal experiences is often unique, the meaning flowing from them is not. We all sense significance in our lives, and we all have our stories to tell.

My hope is that this small volume may inspire you to write and share. Understand that those closest to you may have heard your stories, even stopped listening to them, and if written, may have never read them. No matter. There will be others who will read them, and so I invite you to write for them, and for you.

Acknowledgements

This book arose in large part from years of support by my wife and life companion, Linda. She gave me the space to write, the encouragement to share, and a sense of purpose to celebrate.

This book also arose because of the rich heritage of philosophical discussion in my childhood. As an only child, my principal intellectual mentors were my father, grandfather, and uncle who felt compelled to educate me as they educated themselves in philosophy and economics. Though their education was limited and their ideas not entirely logical or consistent, they were passionate about ideological engagement, and it became a significant influence in my upbringing. I thank them for caring enough to include me. I thank my mother for allowing them to have me, but also for rescuing me when the debates became long and heated, allowing me to escape for normal childhood activities.

Stories about my grandfather (Uncommon Sight) and my uncle (Old Soldiers Never Die) are based on accounts they told me, to the best of my recollection. Quotes in Lazy Summer Days are approximations of the dialogue in my family, and are not represented as actual factual statements. Pilgrimage refers to family genealogical research which remains incomplete and may be flawed. In High School Reunion, I used a fictional name for our host (Tom).

I thank my seventh grade English teacher, whose name I cannot recall, but whose face and affection are forever with me. She saw a kid from a poor, ethnic neighborhood, who struggled to learn English as a second language, who could not write a complete sentence or articulate his thoughts in a tight paragraph. She took the time to teach me after school, one-on-one, how to begin to write concisely and clearly. I am reminded of the scene in *A River Runs Through It* when the writing of the oldest son is critiqued by his father. So it was with me. She gave me both the gift of believing I could write well with practice, and the gift of thinking about my life experiences and writing about them. My final essay in her class was a biographical paper about my father.

There are many friends and teachers who have influenced me along the way, and have given me reason to pause and reflect on life issues. I thank them all, especially Eaton, Peter, Allan, Willie, Maryanne (MJ), Adeline, Ted, Bill, and Josh in whose philosophical circle I reside. They keep me growing.

Lastly, this book would not be in its present form without the editorial work of Lori Stephens of Createspace. Her numerous suggestions and critique were invaluable in helping me to prepare this manuscript.

About the Author...

Steven Mayer, PhD, lives in Eugene, Oregon with his wife, Linda. He is a mostly retired business professional and consultant. Currently, he teaches Human Resource Management in the Lundquist College of Business at the University of Oregon. His intellectual passions include philosophy and the social sciences. His life passions include exploring the natural world, pursuing adventure and travel, and enjoying his children and grandchildren. His favorite hiking companion is his golden retriever, Luke.

Chronology of Writings

ROOTS

Lazy Summer Days (1950-55)

Harvest Time (1950)

Heading South (1951)

His Smile (1958 & 1967)

Uncommon Sight (1968)

Never Look Back (1959)

REMINISCENCES

Such a Thought (1972)

My Littlest Girl (1973)

The First Day (1975)

Summer Evening (1976)

Different Notes (1981)

Going Home Again (1989)

The Old Chestnut Tree

Forgiveness Finally (1984)

Out of the Darkness

Into the Light

Old Soldiers Never Die (1989-2005)

The Gift (2003)

Pilgrimage (2005)

A New Day

Dreamer (1976)

A Few Words for my Grandchildren (1994)

REFLECTIONS

Child Within (1973)

Beauty to Me (1985)

Old Apple Tree to the North (1977-1983)

Wildflowers (1986)

Coming Back (1987)

A Walk in the Rain (1995)

Candlelight (1972)

Listen

Homecoming

On Power

Together

Going Right

A Few Words for my Grandchildren (1994)

RECOGNITIONS

You

Prayer of a Skeptic (1980)

Inside Me

Finding Heart

Believing (1998)

Final Truth

Vital Lies

In Praise of Doubt

Blessing and Curse (2005)

An Old Journal Entry (2005, 1967)

Not to Worry (2007)

High School Reunion (1982)

In Praise of Hope

Bottles in my Cellar (2003)

REVERENCES

Wilderness (1983)

On the Face (1985)

So Much Wonder and Beauty (2000)

Tribute (1999)

Is it Over? (2000)

Strangers (1988)

Her Touch (2009)

At Play (2008)

Her Way Alone (2010)

Flowering (2004)

Wandering Around (2009)

On Poetry

At the Beach (2009)

Infinite Shore

REALIZATIONS

Every Breath is a Miracle (2010)

Romancing Reincarnation (2010)

Smiling at the Darkness (2011)

Best Gifts (2010)

A Final Thought (2012)

Made in the USA
San Bernardino, CA
31 August 2018